COME WITH DADDY

COME WITH DADDY

CHILD MURDER–SUICIDE AFTER FAMILY BREAKDOWN

CAROLYN HARRIS JOHNSON

UWA PUBLISHING

First published in 2005 and reprinted in 2016 by
University of Western Australia Publishing

Crawley, Western Australia 6009
www.uwap.uwa.edu.au

THE UNIVERSITY OF
WESTERN
AUSTRALIA

Publication of this book was made possible with funding assistance from the Department of Community Development Family Domestic Violence Unit, and the Domestic Violence Legal Aid Unit of Legal Aid Western Australia.

If readers find content distressing, please contact your local telephone crisis counselling service.

National Library of Australia

Cataloguing-in-Publication entry:

Johnson, Carolyn Harris, 1946–.Come with daddy: child murder–suicide after family breakdown.

Bibliography.
Includes index.
ISBN 1 920694 42 0/ ISBN 9781920694425

1. Filicide—Australia. 2. Custody of children—Australia.
3. Family violence—Australia. 4. Children—Crimes against—Australia. 5. Suicide
—Australia. I. Title.
(Series: Contemporary issues (Nedlands, W.A)).
364.15230830994

Cover photograph: Cath Muscat
Consultant editor: Janet Mckenzie
Designed by Pages in Action, Melbourne
Typeset in 10.5/13pt Adobe Garamond
Printed by Lightning Source

*This study is dedicated to the innocent children
whose tragic and untimely deaths
are its subject.*

Contents

List of Figures

Acknowledgments

I wish to thank the faculty and staff of the School of Social and Cultural Studies at The University of Western Australia, for their support, and especially my supervisors, Jim Ife and Maria Harries, for their patient guidance and wisdom, which enabled me to complete the research upon which this book is based.

I am also grateful to the following people, who facilitated my access to the data: Chief Judge Michael Holden; Andrew Stout and Paul Kerin of the Family Court of Western Australia; the staff of the CIB Crime Information Centre; the Western Australian Coroner and Glenn Spivey from the Coroner's Office; Ian Vaughan and Jan Broughton from the Department of Justice; Anna Ferrante and David Indermaur from the Crime Research Centre; Vince Jones and Harvey Hatch. at the Victim Support Service; and the staff of the Battye Library of Western Australian History.

I am indebted to Jenny Mouzos at the Australian Institute of Criminology for her excellent advice, and to Maureen de la Harpe, editorial consultant at University of Western Australia Press, for her quiet sensitivity, wisdom, and support throughout the process of turning this research project into a book.

I would also like to thank my friends and colleagues for their support and encouragement throughout this endeavour, particularly my dear friend Helen Hall for her able assistance in formatting the document. Special thanks are due to Anne Moore of the Lucy Saw Women's Refuge, the Women's Council for Domestic and Family Violence Services (WA) and Bev Jowle, Community Development Officer at the Department for Community Development Rockingham,

WA, for their insights which helped to clarify my thoughts on future directions.

My appreciation is also due to my large and wonderful family who don't understand what I do, or why I choose to do it, but always give me their unconditional support anyway. I especially want to thank my son, Matthew, for his encouragement and unfailing belief in me, and my best friend, husband and partner in life, Frank, for his unflagging support throughout this and all my other undertakings, and for his painstaking editing of the early drafts.

Finally, and most importantly, I would like to thank the survivors of familicide who, after experiencing perhaps the biggest breach of trust imaginable, found the courage to share their trauma with an unknown researcher, in the hope that this work would increase our knowledge about the offence of familicide, and help to provide a safer future for the children of other troubled families.

Carolyn Harris Johnson
December 2004

The Stories

This chapter recounts the crimes that are at the heart of this study and describes the victims, the survivors and some characteristics of the offences.

MICHAEL AND NARELLE'S FAMILY

Michael arrived at his wife's house at 6.30 am one morning, four days after Narelle had left him, taking their children with her. He requested access with the two children, aged four and three years. At interview, Narelle indicated she had not wished the children to go with their father, but was not able to refuse access as she felt powerless in the relationship. Her daughter had screamed, because she didn't want to go with her father, but Narelle had encouraged her to go, as she was reportedly fearful of her husband's response should she refuse access.

Michael took the children on this 'agreed' access visit and drove them to the place where he and Narelle used to park as lovers. Here he gave the children whisky in soft drink, to make them sleep, and then gassed them by connecting a hose to the exhaust pipe and placing it into the car. It appears that, as he lost consciousness, he had second thoughts about his actions and pushed open the door to let some air in.

He managed to save himself but the children died. Ultimately he served a lengthy jail sentence for the double homicide of his children, and he now lives in the community with his second wife and their children. It is not clear when he was released from prison, as the maternal family was not formally notified.

Narelle reported that, although she had left the relationship several times before, this time she had been determined that it would be the couple's final separation. There had been no Family Court involvement, and no court order.

Two years later, Family Court records show that Michael applied for a dissolution of the marriage. In the application the children are described as deceased, but there is no mention on the file that the children had been killed by their father, even though his address was recorded as Fremantle Prison.

If Michael's second marriage were to end and an application came before the Family Court, the court would have no record of his previous offence; even if such a record did exist, this information would probably not be available to the judicial officer dealing with the case.

TOM AND CLARE'S FAMILY

After a separation lasting a year, Tom took his two children, aged three years and eighteen months, on an access visit ordered by the court (by Minute of Consent). He and Clare had agreed in the Minute of Consent that his visits should be supervised by a member of his family, either his parents or his sister. The younger child was returned home after this daytime visit with his father, as the court considered him too young for overnight access. Tom was reportedly allowed by his relatives to take his daughter away, unsupervised, in contravention of the court order. He drove to an isolated place, put a hose from the exhaust into the car, and gassed his child and himself to death.

At interview, Clare indicated she had not wanted the children to have any access with their father, as the older child had disclosed her father previously attempted to murder her. Clare believes the court ignored the child's report of the attempted suffocation by her father, and gave it no credibility, because she was only three years of age. Clare also felt very pressured by her lawyer, who had told her she must agree to some form of access, or the court would view her as unreasonable and order access anyway.

Clare reported there had been no legal consequence for the husband's family, although their failure to supervise the contact breached an order of the Family Court. This case had been active in the Family Court for two and a half months following Tom's application for access to his children. In addition, there was a current Minute of Consent, made in the Family Court, dated two months prior to the offence, and a conciliation conference was scheduled to take place a week after the offence occurred.

GARY AND JENNIFER'S FAMILY

Gary and Jennifer had been separated for fourteen months. Their case had gone to a Family Court trial, which was characterised by allegations from both the husband and wife about each other's parenting deficits. There were serious allegations relating to the sexual abuse by Gary of all three children. He picked up the three children, aged five, four and three years, on a court-ordered access visit, took them to an isolated spot in the national forest, and gassed them and himself in his car.

It is evident from the file that there was significant Family Court involvement in this case for some time before the offence, and Jennifer's application for dissolution of marriage, custody and guardianship of the children had been lodged in the court. Documents confirm there had been a long and acrimonious court case, which had proceeded to trial, with both parties not only criticising each other's parenting, but attacking each other's character. This led the presiding judge to remonstrate with both parties for their negative attitudes to one another, and the effect this had on their parenting.

Gary had told a friend before the offence that he would never allow Jennifer to have custody of the children. This information was not passed on to the authorities and therefore could not be used to ensure the children's safety.

PETER AND RITA'S FAMILY

Peter and Rita had been separated for three weeks, and it appears he kept the children and would not hand them over to Rita. Peter abducted his own two children, aged five years and one year, and his stepson aged seven years. The Family Court issued a ruling giving him access with the children two weekends out of every three, but the children were to be returned to their mother who had principal custody of them. After the ruling, Peter told Rita that he would kill the children. He threatened that if she won in court she would ultimately lose, and that he would not allow her to raise the children with another man. An order had been made for Peter to return the children to their mother, which he refused to do. Consequently, a Recovery Order was made when it was known that he had threatened to kill the children. This case had been filed in the Family Court just one week before the offence.

The police were advised of Peter's threats to harm the children, and after locating his vehicle on a country road they gave chase. They abandoned the chase as too dangerous to the children when Peter's vehicle reached a speed of 170 kilometres per hour. After losing the police, Peter drove the children to an isolated place, put a carefully prepared vacuum cleaner hose into the car, and gassed them and himself.

Police located the vehicle too late to save the children or their father. It appeared from scuff marks on the ground outside the car, and bruises and scratches on the bodies of the two older children, that they had struggled to escape, but that their father had used force to restrain them. All three children had been sedated prior to the offence. The coroner described the act as cruel and selfish.

Some years previously, Peter had appeared in the Family Court when he abducted his infant child from a previous marriage after seriously assaulting his first wife when she tried to leave. She had applied to the court for a warrant to have the baby returned to her care. However, no information about the breakdown of this earlier relationship was mentioned in the file on his second marriage, and thus it was not available to decision-makers when his second marriage ended.

MURRAY AND THERESA'S FAMILY

Murray and Theresa had been separated for six weeks. Murray went to Theresa's home before the offence and seriously assaulted her, leaving her bound and gagged. He then went to his children's school where he lured them both away with the promise of gifts.

Murray drove to an isolated spot and gassed the children by placing a hose from the exhaust to the inside of the car. He stabbed them to ensure their death. He then set fire to the car.

Meanwhile, Theresa had freed herself and alerted the police to the abduction of the children. They arrived at the scene to find the car on fire with the children inside. When he saw the police and ambulance arrive, Murray poured turpentine on himself and set himself alight. Both police and ambulance officers suffered burns as they tried to retrieve the children from the burning vehicle and douse the flames engulfing the children's father.

It was not possible to retrieve one child from the burning vehicle. The other was taken to hospital, where she survived for several days before succumbing to her injuries. Murray also survived for several days before dying as a result of his self-inflicted burns.

Prior to his death, Murray was charged with assault occasioning grievous bodily harm for the assault on his wife, and would have been charged with the murder of both children had he survived. This case had no involvement with any process in the Family Court.

PAUL AND ROSEMARY'S FAMILY

Paul and Rosemary had been separated for eight months at the time of the offence, and Paul had his children on a legal contact visit at the time. When he was due to return them to their mother, Paul drove them to an isolated spot in the forest and gassed them and himself in the car.

According to the Family Court file, the couple had used the court to register an agreement on property settlement, child issues relating to residency, guardianship and contact. There was no court appearance by either party, and nothing in the court records to indicate there had been any kind of dispute between them. The whole file consisted of only seven pages, close to the bare minimum for a court file.

Newspapers quoted the police as stating there had been a recent dispute between Paul and Rosemary about access prior to the offence, but no other information was available.

BARRY AND RUTH'S FAMILY

Sixteen months after Ruth had left Barry, she thought he had finally accepted the separation. Then, the evening before the offence, she saw two men pouring something out of a 5-litre can onto the lawn near her house. She rang the police, believing the substance might be petrol and that Barry was attempting to burn her and the children to death. By the time the police came, the two men had departed. As it was raining the police could establish only that there was an oily residue on the lawn, being unable to identify it further. Ruth reported that the police made no investigation and did not attempt to locate and interview Barry, although she believes he was one of the men she saw, nor did they seek to meet or speak with her.

A few hours later, in the early hours of the morning, Barry entered the house by dismantling a toilet window, which he had previously tampered with to facilitate entry. He fatally shot both children as they slept, seriously wounded his wife, and then shot himself. The identity of the second man has never been established. A large amount of money was withdrawn from Barry's account just prior to the offence and has never been found. Ruth believes this money might have been used to pay an accomplice.

Ruth believes that Barry had planned the offence from the time she was served with divorce papers, two months earlier. Supporting this belief was the information that on the day after she signed the papers Barry had purchased a gun from a police officer. She said he had forged a letter to enable him to make the purchase.

Barry had lodged the case in the Family Court. He applied for a divorce, proposing to the court that Ruth have custody of the children. She had wanted him to have regular access, but he had initially refused saying the visits were too painful for him. Access had become regular only in the month preceding the offence.

PREMEDITATION

All persons interviewed believed the offences were premeditated; there is much evidence to support this and no evidence to the contrary. In one case it appears that the offence may even have been rehearsed.

Clare said, 'I know he planned it. He was planning it for a long time. Looking back now I was too stressed. I couldn't see the big picture.' She recalled that after the offence people she knew received recorded audio tapes, which Tom had sent before committing the offence. 'He sent photos of me breast-feeding to all my friends and my employer got one as well.'

Barry committed the only familicide offence that did not occur in public open space, which took place in the family home. He prepared entry for himself beforehand, and it appears had planned to burn down the house as well as murdering his family. He had bought a firearm, providing a forged letter in order to get a licence for it, before shooting his ex-wife, the children and himself. Ruth discovered afterwards that Barry had made plans to carry out the offence for some time. She said:

> It was premeditated. He organised entry, when he returned he dismantled the inside of the toilet window [he had tampered with it on the previous occasion]. It was premeditated, from the time he was served with the divorce papers. He bought a gun the day after he received the documents, and licensed it the next day.

Several women reported their husbands had purchased hoses and substances to sedate the children prior to committing the offence, which suggests the offences were not spontaneous. Danni, an aunt of two of the children, reported the perpetrator had sedated the children with alcohol mixed with a popular soft drink before gassing them. 'He laced Fanta with whisky. He knew what he was doing.'

Peter had carefully prepared garden ties to restrain the children if necessary, and had been observed by a neighbour making an elaborate adaptation to a vacuum hose the day before the offence to ensure its efficiency when used.

As discussed previously, it appears Tom had rehearsed the crime, and the three-year-old disclosed that he had tried to smother her. However, as we have seen, she was not believed; when Tom said she had choked on a biscuit he was given the benefit of the doubt and allowed to continue contact. As her mother reported afterwards: 'She was only three, but she knew the difference between a pillow and a biscuit'.

Murray had, it seems, attempted to stop Theresa raising the alarm or rescuing the children by tying her up and gagging her before abducting the children from school. Paul demonstrated a typical, thorough plan to kill his children and himself, preparing a shopping list for sedatives and a hosepipe before abducting his children. Michael drove the children several hundred kilometres to a very significant and carefully chosen place, which he and their mother had frequented as lovers. He had purchased alcohol and a hosepipe before committing the offence.

Although there was a variety of evidence that the perpetrator intended to kill his ex-partner, this did not actually occur in any of the cases studied. As seen, one woman survived what might have been a serious attempt to kill her; more likely, it was an extremely violent retaliation to punish her for leaving and ensure she survived to experience the pain of her children's demise.

THE VICTIMS

In the seven families studied, fifteen children were murdered, eight girls and seven boys. Their ages ranged from seventeen months to eight years. (Fourteen were killed by their fathers and one was killed by the stepfather who had raised him from infancy.) Among the seven men, there were six suicides and one attempted suicide.

Ruth, the mother who was shot, survived but sustained serious injury as a result of the shooting. She spent many months in hospital undergoing treatment for her injuries, which have left her permanently disabled. Although Barry is known to have threatened to kill her just before the offence, it cannot be known for certain what his intent was. His motivation remains unclear. The shooting occurred at such close range that, had he wanted to kill her, he could easily have done so.

In contrast to the majority of filicides, with the exception of one child, the perpetrator was the biological father of the victims. In the one case where a spouse was seriously injured, the couple were divorced.

THE SURVIVORS

Only one child managed to survive his father's offence. Because he was considered too young to go on an overnight access visit, he was returned to his mother after a short daytime contact, whereas his older sister was deemed able to cope with extended access. The length of time required to drive to an isolated spot without the absence being detected, and then complete the offence undisturbed, apparently saved the younger child's life. The police advised Clare that their investigation had shown Tom had originally intended to kill her and the younger child as well.

Of the seven women in this study, it is not known whether two of them were the subject of death threats or not. Five women were threatened with death by their partners on at least one occasion, either before or after separation. We can only hypothesise why these threats were not realised. The woman who was shot was never told by those in contact with her husband just before the offence that he had threatened to kill her, and the threats were not reported to the police either. In the case where the man left much written and tape-recorded evidence of his thoughts before the offence, the police reportedly advised his wife afterwards that it had clearly been his intention to murder her also. She explained:

> He had a tape for me. It was named 'My Pain'. 'Patience' by Guns 'N' Roses [a popular rock band at the time]. was the song playing at the start of the tape, then he started talking. The detectives have

it. He left me a diary of the whole event. The police won't let me see it. He sat and watched until the last breath went out of her little face. They [the detectives] have the diary. They thought her brother and I would have died as well.

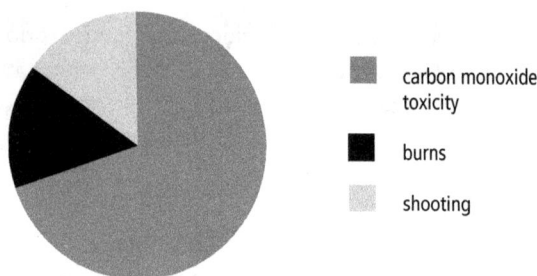

- carbon monoxide toxicity
- burns
- shooting

FIGURE 1: Cause of death, perpetrator

Source: Johnson (2002)

CAUSE OF DEATH

The cause of death in the study population varied significantly from that in comparable violent deaths in Australia such as suicide, spousal homicide and filicide. The majority of perpetrators died from carbon monoxide toxicity (Figure 1), whereas the most common form of male suicide in Australia is hanging or strangulation (Australian Bureau of Statistics 2002a). Of the six successful suicides, four died from carbon monoxide toxicity, one from self-inflicted burns, and one from a self-inflicted gunshot wound. The man who survived his suicide attempt had chosen carbon monoxide as his means.

The only woman who was injured in this study was shot. In Australia, shooting is the second most common form of spousal homicide. The primary method is sharp instrument such as a knife (36 per cent), followed closely by firearm (30 per cent) (Easteal 1993: 36).

Figure 2 shows that the most frequent cause of death of the children in this study was carbon monoxide toxicity. Eleven children were killed in this way. In all cases their fathers attached some type of hose from the car exhaust to the interior of the vehicle and blocked all

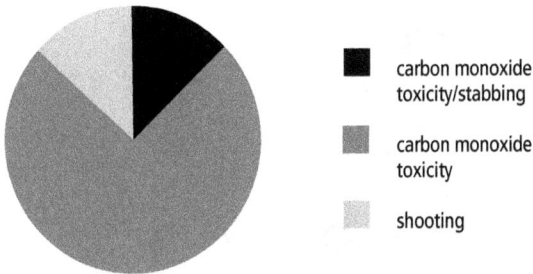

FIGURE 2: Cause of death, children

Source: Johnson (2002)

ventilation. Then they ran the motor, with themselves and the children inside, until the car ran out of petrol and all the occupants expired. The survivors believed that in most cases the children were sedated with drugs or alcohol before their death. This mode of filicide differs markedly from that in the thirteen-year Australian study by Mouzos and Rushforth, which found forceful assault to be responsible for 46 per cent of filicide deaths and a knife or other sharp instrument for 13 per cent (2003: 4).

Two children died from a combination of carbon monoxide toxicity and stabbing, although they also suffered serious burns. In this case their father had first gassed them in his car and then stabbed them to ensure death. It is not clear why this man chose also to set fire to the vehicle, unless it was to prevent the police from rescuing the children at the last minute. Two children were shot by their father at point-blank range while sleeping in their mother's bed in their own home.

Children are always vulnerable and relatively defenceless against an adult who may wish to harm them. Carbon monoxide poisoning is unfortunately fairly easy to effect with young children although, as we have seen, in one case two older children apparently struggled with their father outside the vehicle and sustained bruising as a result. It appears from this they may have been aware of his intention, but his superior strength overcame them and they died alongside him and their baby sister.

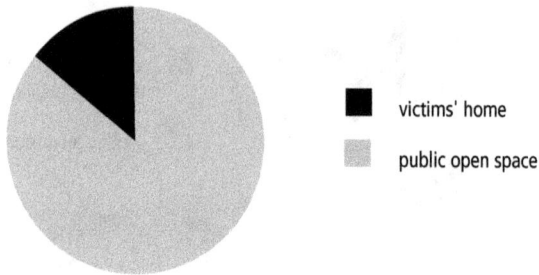

FIGURE 3: Location of offence

Source: Johnson (2002)

CHARACTERISTICS OF THE OFFENCE

Previous research finds that the family home is the most common venue in both spousal homicide and filicide. In contrast, the familicides in this study, with one exception, occurred in public open space such as bushland or a national forest (Figure 3).

The only case where the offence occurred in the woman's home was also the only case where the woman was seriously injured. All the other offences occurred in very isolated locations. It is obvious all the perpetrators had carefully chosen these locations, where they were almost certain to evade notice until they had completed the offence.

The time of day at which death occurred could not be established in all cases, although five of the police reports mention when the bodies were discovered. In these cases the time of discovery ranged from 2.36 am to 7.05 pm. As most of the offences took place in public space, the bodies were most likely to be discovered during daylight hours by recreational users of the area.

Three offences occurred on weekdays and the date of one could not be determined. The offences were spread throughout the year: two in January, one each in June, July, August and September, and one in December. Three occurred within a week or so of the traditional holiday period between Christmas and New Year (Figure 4). It is likely that feelings of loss may be worse at this time of year for individuals

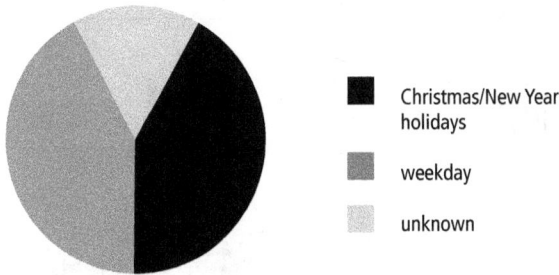

FIGURE 4: When offence occurred

Source: Johnson (2002)

who are having difficulty coping with separation, because there are constant reminders about the joys of family life and the special meaning of Christmas to small children. Moreover, non-custodial parents generally share an extended period with their children during the holidays; after enjoying this special time, they may feel extreme distress at having to return them to the custodial parent.

It could be said that certain times of year might heighten the risk for some families. Another view is that the perpetrator's perception of the spousal relationship, and his control, or lack of it, over what he considers to be 'his' family unit, are far more important in determining the time of highest risk (Ewing 1997: 22–4; Polk 1994: 189).

SUMMARY

Of the seven offences, a total of twenty-one people died and three survived. Two people survived an actual homicide attempt. The only child that survived has suffered long-term psychological and behavioural problems. Michael, the only surviving perpetrator, continues to seek contact with his ex-wife. Although her family continue to protect her, they fear he will eventually find her. The trauma to the surviving members of the maternal and paternal extended families cannot be measured.

The Study

As a mature-age social work graduate, I worked for more than ten years in the criminal justice system, most of it in high-security men's prisons. Thus I met individuals whose life experiences were in many cases characterised by various forms of deprivation and abuse. The offences they had committed had brought pain and trauma not only to the victims and their families and associates, but also to their own families and to those who had to deal with the aftermath—police, health workers, court officers and prison officers.

Prisoners' life stories are often poignant. Some of their attempts to overcome their negative experiences and find dignity and a sense of purpose for themselves are courageous, even heroic. Those few who hear these stories can be just as moved by them as they are by the details surrounding the offences themselves. At times I felt humbled by this experience. Indeed, my reaction to one man's experience provided the impetus for me to undertake this study.

This man was serving a sentence for murdering his two young children, and afterwards he had attempted suicide several times. The offence occurred while he was suffering from an undiagnosed psychiatric illness, and it followed a marital separation that he had not been able to cope with. During the period of separation and the litigation in the Family Court, he had access to counselling and psychiatric assessment and treatment. From the evidence provided in the public domain about his behaviour, there were signs of deterioration in his mental health prior to the offence. However, these signs were either not recognised, or not acted upon, and therefore he was able to plan and undertake his crime unhindered.

Throughout this man's incarceration he remained severely clinically depressed, remorseful and often suicidal. I counselled him, as did several of my colleagues, over many years as he moved through the prison system, from maximum security to medium, then to minimum, and finally to an open setting.

At the time of his release, it appeared that he had gained some understanding of how he came to commit these offences. However, from the interviews I conducted with him, it seems that he never forgave himself, or overcame his overwhelming shame and remorse. He described each day as an emotional nightmare, in which not only did he have to live with the sense of personal loss and guilt, and the knowledge that he had caused unbearable suffering to the children's mother and the extended family and friends, but he also had to deal with the punitive treatment meted out to him by a small number of prisoners and prison officers. It appeared to him that these people took a perverse pleasure in taunting him about his offences. He would sometimes be left standing at a gate waiting to pass to another area of the prison while prison officers, instead of using his name, referred to him as 'the child killer' or 'the murderer'. In spite of this, he reported that nothing anyone could call him could match the deep loathing he held for himself and for the offence he had committed. His serious attempts to end his life were intended to end his constant emotional torment, caused by the realisation of what he had done, and the knowledge that he would never be free from it.

By any measure, the crimes this man committed were extremely violent, and yet it was reported that he had loved his children. Those who knew him said that he doted on the children and did his best to provide them with all the things which he had been deprived of as a child. My contact with this man had a profound effect on me, and left questions that neither I nor my colleagues were able to answer. The questions were: 'How could such a tragedy occur?' and 'What could professionals or other community members have done to help prevent it?'

These questions remained unanswered when I later found myself working in the Family Court Counselling Service. Some male clients, deeply distressed over a relationship breakdown, would talk about killing their children or their ex-partner, while contemplating their own suicide. Women did not appear to harbour these thoughts—or if they did, they chose not to articulate them. It often appeared that the men who spoke of killing themselves and their families viewed their wives and their children as an extension of themselves, rather than as individuals in their own right. They appeared to me to be unable to differentiate between their own emotional responses to the marital separation, and those of their children. When challenged about their homicidal thoughts, the men would seem surprised, and would often respond by assuring me that they would never hurt their children. Once more I was faced with the paradoxical coexistence of parental love and homicidal violence.

When I decided to undertake this study, it was clear that I would not find the answer to this baffling offence by interviewing the perpetrators, because few of them survived their suicide attempt. Therefore, I decided to use a combination of document searches and interviews of surviving family members. I hoped to gain an initial understanding about what was happening in these families in the lead-up to the offences, and perhaps shed some light on what motivated men (for this type of offence is rarely committed by women) to commit them. Such information could then pave the way for future research.

FAMILICIDE

It is extremely doubtful whether descriptions of violence that deal only with the personal characteristics of the perpetrator really help us to understand the causes of child murder. Such explanations, though, are rife in both popular and professional discussions of murder and are couched in simplistic psychological and sexual terms (Wilson 1985: 7).

When marital relationships break down, couples are usually able to determine which parent the children should live with, and how frequently and under what circumstances the children should see the other parent. Even in cases where parents initially disagree about these matters, it seems most are eventually able to put their children's needs before their own and resolve any disputes.

In a few cases, however, following a marital separation where the parents have disputed custody and access, the non-custodial parent (most often the father) kills the children and himself. Homicide of this kind is almost always followed by the suicide or attempted suicide of the perpetrator. This type of homicide–suicide is referred to in the literature as 'familicide' (see Glossary). It causes not only the death of young children, but also resultant distress to families, paramedics, officers of the court, legal practitioners and other members of the community. Somewhere in Australia, almost every year, children die as a result of familicide. The anguish and trauma that these offences cause to families, to individuals within agencies providing services to them, and to communities, persist long after the event.

There has been little research into familicide, so professionals do not understand the problem sufficiently to be able to say how, or why, these offences occur. Therefore, it has not been possible to hypothesise about how they might be prevented. The study outlined here examined a number of cases of familicide that occurred in Western Australia following marital separation, and its aim was to determine whether common factors could be identified among them. If such factors could be identified, they might increase our understanding of the dynamics of these offences, establish why they occur, and assist in identifying families at risk. The next step would be to devise strategies to prevent such crimes occurring. Thus, the study was intended to help to fill the existing gaps in the knowledge about familicide and, importantly, to provide a basis for further research.

In attempting to understand the offence of familicide, it is useful to consider the wider context of homicide generally. Homicide is not a common offence in Australia. The rate remains fairly static at approximately 1.9 per 100,000 population (Strang 1993: 12; Mouzos and Rushforth 2003: 32). As it is usual for homicide to be perpetrated against a single victim, and as the incidence of homicide is relatively low, cases of multiple homicide cause a dramatic increase in the homicide statistics.

When a homicide includes multiple victims, whether adults or children, there is frequently a familial relationship between the offender and the victims, and these offences are followed by the suicide of the perpetrator much more frequently than in cases where the relationship between perpetrator and victim is more distant, or where there is no relationship (Daly and Wilson 1988: 217). Child murder almost always occurs in the context of the family. Cases of more than one child being killed at the same time are particularly unusual, but when this does occur the offence is usually followed by the suicide of the perpetrator. Whatever psychological disturbance or negative social experiences the perpetrator may have suffered, and whatever events occurred before the offence took place, homicide remains the ultimate crime of violence. When the victim is a child, the offence is all the more disturbing because children are vulnerable and have an intrinsic right to be protected from harm by all adults, but particularly by their parents.

As I have said, very little is known about familicide in general. Even less is known about familicide that occurs within the context of an apparent dispute about custody of and/or access to children. It follows that there is no information about the background of the perpetrators or the circumstances preceding the offence. Separate statistics on this type of familicide are not available in Australia and do not appear to be available elsewhere either. Where information is available, it is usually found in the literature on domestic violence or spousal homicide.

In cases of familicide, newspapers often quote the opinions of police, family members, or acquaintances of the perpetrator and victims, in an attempt to explain it. Occasionally, professional opinion is sought in an attempt to throw some light on the causes. Explanations seldom cover the complexities of the offence—either the events preceding the crime or the motivation of the perpetrator.

In Western Australia, as in the rest of the country, these offences occur occasionally in cases where sexual intimates have separated and there is reportedly a dispute about custody or access. At these times, typically, the media criticise the Family Court for its decision-making processes, because often these events are associated with divorce or child custody proceedings. Some people apparently believe that fathers are treated unfairly in the Family Court, and that the frustration they feel as a result is a major contributor to familicide.

Some media reports suggest these offences are premeditated, and that they occur after months or years of dysfunctional behaviour by the perpetrator, including threats to harm himself and other family members. Such reports are consistent with my findings.

The Family Court has been involved in a number of cases where the access (or non-custodial) parent has murdered a child or children; threatened, attempted to murder, or murdered their ex-spouse; and then suicided or attempted suicide. In almost every known familicide of this type, where custody or contact with children was seen to be in dispute, including the cases in this study, the perpetrator of the offence was a man—either the father or, in exceptional cases, the stepfather of the children. 'An infrequent but regular variety of homicide is that in which a man destroys his wife and children. A corresponding act of familicide by the wife is almost unheard of' (Daly and Wilson 1988: 82).

In contrast, where women murder and then commit suicide, the research suggests there is usually evidence of delusional thought processes such as psychotic depression or schizophrenia (West 1965: 163). Typically, the woman believes that she, her partner, and her children are to be overtaken by some horrific fate, and that killing them and herself is an act of mercy. This is not usually the case when the perpetrator is a man. In the latter cases, the offences more usually follow a separation initiated by the wife, which the man had difficulty accepting (Daly and Wilson 1992, cited in Hore, Gibson and Bordow 1996: 10). There are often reports of the male's rage, proprietary attitude, or obsessive jealousy in response to the loss of the relationship. It could be argued that few women actually lose custody of their children as a result of Family Court proceedings, or as a result of separation or divorce generally. However, from the literature on spousal homicide and family killings, it is apparent that the human cost of these offences is immense and probably immeasurable. For this reason it is important for us to gain better understanding of the offence, through which we can work towards prevention.

I worked as a Family Court counsellor for a number of years. During this time I observed that parents who had matters before the court after an unrelated familicide had occurred often became anxious. Duty counsellors at the Family Court Counselling Service would hear distressed clients refer to these incidents. Sometimes frustrated non-custodial fathers commented that they could understand men being driven to kill their children, and themselves, after experiencing marital separation that significantly reduced their contact with their children. They would express compassion and understanding for the perpetrator of these offences, and occasionally make veiled threats to commit such an offence themselves. In contrast, women would express fear about their own or their children's safety, especially where they believed their ex-partner was not coping emotionally with the separation, and where he had threatened in the past to hurt his ex-partner, the children, or himself. Throughout this study, I found that when women expressed their fears the community did not respond appropriately, and the danger to the children was either ignored or minimised.

It is accepted that perpetrators of other violent offences, such as rape and assault, have common factors in their psychosocial histories (Ewing 1997: 23; Jenkins 1993: 53–4; Finkelhor and Araji 1986, cited in Jenkins 1993: 23). It was not known prior to the study being undertaken whether there were also common factors in familicide.

DESIGN OF THE STUDY

The study was exploratory and descriptive because of the lack of information on familicide. The method used for the research was a collective case study. This methodology was chosen for several reasons. Firstly, such case studies are appropriate when 'it is believed that understanding them will lead to better understanding, perhaps better theorising, about a still larger collection of cases' (Denzin and Lincoln 1994: 237). Secondly, it suited the small number of cases and the expected difficulties in contacting family members to conduct an in-depth interview. Thirdly, such an approach can include data from a range of other sources, as well as in-depth interviews.

The research combined interviews with survivors and documentary analysis. Each case was selected on the basis that custody of and/or access to children seemed to be in dispute at the time of the offence. As the study progressed this matter became questionable. Indeed, not one of the survivors interviewed believed there had been a current dispute about custody or access at the time the offence was committed. Initially, this led to difficulties engaging respondents because they did not believe they fitted the criteria of the study. Even so, document searches indicated there had been arguments, or even legal dispute, between most of the parents at some time following separation, if not at the time of the offence. Within the terms of this study, however, it now seems unlikely that such a dispute had a causal relationship to the homicide-suicide event, for reasons that will become apparent.

Population, Scope and Data

Originally, I intended to limit the study to the ten years from 1989 to 1999, and include all cases of familicide that had occurred in Western Australia during this time where disputed custody or access had been a factor. However, when my attention was drawn to two cases that fell outside that time frame I incorporated them, believing that an increase in the number of cases from five to seven would maximise the opportunity for understanding to learn and that this was more important than retaining the original time frame.

Because there were so few cases of familicide in the defined circumstances, it was not necessary, nor would it have been possible, to construct a sample. I attempted to contact all the families where this type of familicide had been committed, but contact was not always possible and the numbers were limited by availability. Therefore, I interviewed only four survivors from the seven families, and no perpetrators. Due to the sensitive nature of the research topic, I had to be especially considerate in my method of approach. In each case I made contact through a third party, either the Victim Support Service or another survivor.

The study attempted to see what, if any, characteristics were common among the seven cases selected. For the two cases that had occurred prior to 1989, some of the relevant details about the offence were not available because they preceded the establishment of the police database to which I had access. However, these two cases did provide a wealth of information, which was by and large consistent with the five cases first selected. No doubt other cases occurred before 1989 that would have met the criteria, but I could not access any at the time of the study.

It was extremely difficult to obtain information. Sometimes months passed while I waited for approval to access records, which subsequently yielded little or no useful data. Sometimes potentially rich sources of accessible information, such as old newspaper records, required painstaking hours of research for surprisingly little result.

I used a combination of document searches and survivor interviews to collect the data. The interviews provided accounts of the experiences of survivors, which I believe are critical to understanding the phenomenon of familicide. Document searches were expansive. The Crime Information Centre of the Western Australian Police Service provided access to homicide records, while other sources were various Western Australian newspaper archives, Family Court of Western Australia files, including the records of the Counselling Service, and data from the Coroner's Office. I searched these sources to determine the official cause of death of the victims, to confirm the demographics and to obtain extra information about the offence.

I also accessed Department of Justice records to try to locate any perpetrators who might have survived a suicide attempt. To do this I had to gain permission from the then Ministry of Justice's Research Committee, because perpetrators were obviously vulnerable to the media if the research were to be published. As most homicides attract considerable media attention, it is not uncommon for interest in the offence to be revived when the perpetrator is released into society. Such interest, occurring at such a stressful time for the prisoner, may reduce prospects of rehabilitation. It took several attempts and, finally, referral to a separate and superordinate committee, to gain approval to look at these records.

To gain information about the first-hand experience of survivors, I interviewed three mothers of the murdered children, and one other relative. They were the only survivors of the seven offences whom I was able to locate.

I determined the broad areas I would examine after searching the literature on familicide, homicide, child homicide and suicide. I relied particularly on the literature about spousal homicide, which appears to have similar characteristics to familicide. The review of the literature helped me to devise questions that looked to be relevant to the topic. I then formed these questions into a schedule or interview guide (see Appendix 3), which I used when interviewing the survivors to give some structure within and consistency across interviews.

I mixed open-ended questions with closed questions, but the majority were open-ended as this allowed me to fully explore the respondents' perception of events. Closed questions were primarily used to establish facts, such as whether or not the individuals were involved in a court process at the time of the offence, the age of family members, and whether the parents were legally married or in a de facto relationship.

Ethical Issues

The study required contact with people who had been subject to trauma, in addition to very sensitive data about the deaths, by murder, of young children and infants. It was therefore necessary to gain approval from the research committees that oversee access to the data relating to the offences. I obtained permission from five separate ethics committees, a process that took many months.

There were also ethical issues associated with approaching and interviewing survivors because of the traumatic nature of the event and my lack of knowledge about the individual's coping mechanisms, support systems and access to, or progress in, therapy. It was therefore essential that agreement to participate in the study be based on informed consent. Accordingly, participants were asked to provide written consent (see Appendix 2) in which they were advised of a complaints procedure. I also provided them with an information sheet (see Appendix 1), which explained why the research was being under-taken, warned that participation in the study might cause them distress, and advised where support could be obtained, if needed, following the interview.

I had to consider the effect on the survivor of discussing the offence, because the questions asked could stimulate memories that would undoubtedly be painful. Thus, it was incumbent upon me, as the researcher, to be alert for and recognise trauma responses when they arose, and to respond sensitively to them.

Understandably, it took a good deal of courage for survivors to meet a total stranger and talk about their most personal and devastating tragedy. In most cases I did not simply make an appointment, meet the survivor and conduct the interview. More often the interviewees can-celled (often at the last minute) and appointments were rescheduled several times before taking place. Sometimes I travelled long distances (on one occasion 600 kilometres) to find that the interviewee simply did not show up. The reasons given for non-attendance varied from a misunderstanding about the date or the time to 'It's not a good day today'. All the survivors were aware that in meeting and talking, they would relive their experience, and the effect of doing so would be extremely painful not just on the day of the interview but for some considerable time afterwards. For days or weeks after the interview I received telephone calls or letters providing additional information, because talking about their experience led survivors to remember addi-tional aspects of the event which they had forgotten, and which they wanted included in the research.

I learnt, by my own omission, how important it is that the researcher remain available to respondents, even months after the initial contact, by supplying a current telephone number. Respondents may need to ask questions about the study, or wish to verify information previously provided to them, especially with regard to confidentiality. When the researcher is unavailable, respondents may be caused unnec-essary anxiety and distress.

All survivors interviewed showed great courage in participating and, universally, did so out of a desire to contribute to the knowledge in this area. They were all well aware that little is known about the phenomenon of familicide. They talked about wanting to assist by providing information in the hope that familicide could be better understood, and hopefully thus contribute to a reduction in future incidents. They were interested not only in prevention, but also in the improvement of services to families. They reported significant gaps in services, or even a total absence of them—both before the offence, when they were experiencing difficulties in separating from their partners, and afterwards, when they needed help to cope with the resultant trauma.

Homicide Data and Records

In Western Australia, the computerised family homicide data that were available at the time of this study categorised perpetrator–victim relationships only to the extent that there was a relationship. The specific nature of that relationship, be it father, mother, brother, spouse, was only obtainable by examining the offence reports of these homicides. To do this, I had to approach The University of Western Australia's Crime Research Centre, which collects the homicide data, and request the offence numbers for all familial homicides. The police then provided a list of all relevant offence reports, which I examined individually to determine which of them met the criteria of the study

Offence reports are stored at the headquarters of the Criminal Investigation Bureau. They are very brief, giving only basic information about each offence. They generally do not give much background and in some cases do not state the ultimate fate of the perpetrator. In murder–suicide the coroner's office undertakes the investigation because there is no surviving offender for police to charge. In cases where the police arrived at the crime scene and the perpetrator was still alive following a suicide attempt, the offence report did not state whether or not he ultimately survived.

While collecting the police data, I was not allowed to record the names of the perpetrators or victims, and later had to search newspaper archives around the offence date to ascertain who the families were. From the offence reports I could ascertain the relationship of each murder victim to the perpetrator and the age and sex of the victims, although I was not able to determine in every case that the offence was a familicide related to a dispute about custody or access.

The Western Australian Ministry of Justice authorised access to prisoners' records, subject to the usual ethical and confidentiality considerations. I sought permission to see whether any perpetrators had survived to be charged, tried and sentenced, because, as I have said, this was not always clear from newspaper archives or police records. It is common for murderers to attempt suicide, sometimes successfully, after the offence while on remand or serving a sentence in jail. However, a review of offender management data revealed there were no surviving perpetrators serving a prison sentence.

In order to locate and interview survivors I needed the families' names. I tried to obtain them in the Western Australian State Library archives of the state's newspapers, including daily, weekend and rural publications. I checked in the microfilm records all issues of newspapers for two weeks after the date on which each offence was discovered. This took many hours and at first was relatively fruitless as only two names came to light. I was extremely disappointed, but fortunately the Coroner's Office produced more information, which enabled me to obtain the remaining names. Then I returned to the newspaper archives to find out more.

Victim Support Service

The Victim Support Service routinely contacts all victims of violent crime to offer counselling, support, information and other resources. When I approached it asking for assistance to contact survivors, I learnt that many victims do not choose to use the service. The service does not necessarily follow up initial contacts in case this is construed as harassment, especially when survivors are in an extremely vulnerable state. However, the service was helpful and raised the topic of the research with its Homicide Survivors Group, encouraging survivors of familicide to contact me. At that time only one member was a survivor of familicide, and she subsequently contacted me and agreed to be interviewed. The Victim Support Service also allowed me to address its counsellors on the research topic, and ask if they would approach any other clients who they knew were survivors to request their participation. By this means I located another survivor, who was not involved with the group but agreed to be interviewed. It was this woman who told me about the two cases falling outside the study time frame.

Initially, all these respondents declined involvement when they heard the topic of the research, because they believed their cases did not involve any conflict about custody or access. This may have been because respondents believed that no court involvement indicated no dispute, as already mentioned, but it may relate to the fact that the dispute was not really about custody or access, but more about the rejection or abandonment experienced by the perpetrator.

Attempts to Locate Other Respondents

Efforts were made to locate other survivors, but at this point it seemed they had all vanished and could not be found. Then a colleague mentioned that she had been involved with a family where familicide had occurred. I approached the agency of which this woman had been a client, seeking permission to access her address and contact her. However, the agency refused permission on the grounds that it was not known how the woman was coping with the trauma of the offence and that my contact might reactivate the trauma. Therefore unfortunately this case could not be included in the study.

One woman, who had already been interviewed, provided the name and address of another survivor, who she believed would wish to participate in the study. I wrote to this address but the letter was eventually returned to sender, and so this case also had to be omitted from the study.

Analysing the Information

I opened a working file to track the various details of the cases, adding more information as I collected it. Gradually, I pieced together the relevant data from the various sources.

Sensitivity dictated that the survivors be given the opportunity to choose the place of interview, a place where they would feel most comfortable and safe. Interestingly, two nominated their own homes and two a neutral place. The length of interviews varied greatly. Usually, the longer the interview the more detail was revealed, and the more evident became the distress of the respondents. The interviews were intensely emotional, and I found it impossible to work immediately on the information obtained because it was so distressing to read. I had to allow some time to elapse before undertaking any further interview.

I grouped the information gained from the interviews under appropriate headings, so the antecedents to the offence, the offence itself, and the aftermath appeared in a sequential format, rather than as individual case studies. I believed this method of presentation would help to preserve anonymity for respondents.

Initially, the primary focus of the research was on the family's experience of the Family Court, and the perpetrator's history of domestic violence and mental illness. However, as the interviews developed, it became apparent that common themes were emerging. The research therefore identifies how families responded to the tragedy of their children's murders; what the long-term effects have been on the families and the individuals involved; and the availability of services to families before and after the event.

It turned out most of the families in the study had had some contact with a range of community agencies. Were the workers involved with them aware of the risk factors? If not, why not? If they were aware, why weren't these offences prevented? These questions are important, as their answers will point to the directions needed for change in policies and practice. Survivors reported long histories of victimisation and abuse, and some of the women had contacted police numerous times for help. They reported feeling their concerns were either not heard, or were ignored, by police, lawyers, and the courts. One woman believed that her own lawyer had filtered out information relating to her husband's violence before the case reached the court. Underscoring the findings of other studies relating to domestic violence and spousal homicide (Easteal 1993: 182; Hore, Gibson and Bordow 1996), my study showed that Restraining Orders are virtually useless in protecting women and children from violent husbands and fathers.

Each of the perpetrators in this study was male, the father or stepfather of the children, and was aged between twenty-seven and thirty-nine years. The couples were either married or de facto partners, but all were living separately at the time of the offence. The victims were the children and one of the mothers. The survivors are the mothers, siblings, aunts, uncles, grandparents and friends of the murdered children. The survivors interviewed were the mothers and, in one case, a maternal relative of the murdered children.

As noted, it was not possible to make any contact with a perpetrator although I attempted to do so. Families of perpetrators are even harder to contact than survivors because no services are provided specifically for them. Given that these families also include the victims, this was an unexpected finding. The parents of perpetrators have lost not only their grandchildren to homicide, but also their son to suicide—or, in the rare case the man survives and is imprisoned for his offences, to a lengthy period of incarceration. Imprisonment causes great emotional hardship to most families of offenders, but when the offence is family homicide this distress is much worse. These families are left to cope with their loss, grief, shame and, no doubt, guilt, with very little support.

CONSTRAINTS OF THE STUDY

I had hoped to interview a surviving perpetrator, and I made contact with a man who agreed to consider participating in the study. But then a familicide occurred involving five children where the perpetrator was the children's mother. Although this offence was not related to separation and disputed custody or access, the emotional impact on the man was so great that he withdrew from the study. Despite my disappointment, I accepted that the nature of this type of research means that trauma, and its reactivation, is a constant factor which cannot be controlled.

There were initial problems in tracking down survivors, due to their understandable need for privacy or wish to shun publicity. When contact was made, trust had to be established before proceeding to the interview stage. As mentioned above, the survivors showed some reluctance to participate due to their belief they were not suitable, as they had no disagreement about custody or access. Two women had had current Consent Orders as a result of an agreement reached with their ex-partners in the Family Court. The others had never been to court and believed there was no disagreement about their ex-partners' contact with the children.

Due to the lack of available information about the families of perpetrators or their whereabouts, I could not include data from the paternal side of the murdered children's families. Thus I have not been able to present the paternal families' perspective on the offence, the events which led up to it, or the aftermath. This lack of perspective, coupled with the absence of the perpetrators' voices, leaves a large gap in the research. Hopefully this can be filled by future researchers, although they will find it difficult. In many cases the perpetrator has committed suicide, and the lack of specific services available to the perpetrators' families denies the researcher an avenue for contact.

Some of the information in the study is necessarily very subjective and collected from respondents who are clearly still suffering trauma reactions related to the offences. It cannot be known to what extent this has affected the information.

SUMMARY

This study pieced together the events preceding each of the selected familicide incidents in order to gain information that would lead to understanding of the complexity of these offences. Although data was not easy to find and I had to locate it in a number of different ways, I believe that the effort was worthwhile because the resulting data was much richer than if it had been sourced from one or two places. It was a challenge to gain approval from so many ethics bodies, but given the sensitive nature of the topic it was to be expected.

From the data gathered, it can be said that there appear to be some major consistencies both in the personalities of the perpetrators and in the way they viewed their partners and children. The survivors, when located, made a huge contribution to the study, although they knew that the experience could be intensely distressing for them. I recognise that they did so for purely altruistic motives, and I hope that they will feel their participation was worthwhile.

It is not possible to clearly define how many survivors there were of the seven offences. The interviewees saw their whole extended family as survivors, and described children born into the family years after the offence as being seriously affected by it. Obviously, as perpetrators' families could not be found, the number of survivors within them could not be determined. Two additional deaths in families were believed to have been caused by the trauma. Both were by heart attack; one was in a maternal family and the other was reported in a paternal family.

Seven women, the ex-partners of the perpetrators, survived. One child, of the sixteen children belonging to the seven couples, survived. One woman received serious injuries as a result of her ex-husband shooting her. It is not clear whether this was attempted murder, or whether, as she believes, he intended that she should survive to suffer the painful experience of her children's murder. However, the term 'survivor' could well include all members of both maternal and paternal families, and could doubtless run into scores if not hundreds of individuals. Fifteen children were murdered: eight girls and seven boys, all aged between one and seven years. One man survived his suicide attempt, but he could not be found to be interviewed; six men committed suicide.

Ideally the implications for policy and practice which flow from this study will receive an appropriate response so that the human cost of these tragedies can be eliminated, or at least minimised. Then the pain and trauma of the maternal and paternal families, police, ambulance officers, medical staff, lawyers, court officers, members of the judiciary, social workers, psychologists, refuge workers and counsellors will not have been in vain, but will have served to focus the community's attention on a serious social problem that needs urgent action.

CHAPTER — 3

The People

> Whatever its origin, homicidal violence directed toward a
> family member is widely regarded as the most dreadful and
> frightening of all crimes. Killing a family member seems
> especially horrible because families are—at least according to
> popular myth—warm, loving, peaceful social units, the members
> of which loyally defend, protect, and nurture one another
> (Ewing 1987: 11).

Information about the families in the study is presented here to provide
an authentic context for the offences, but I have minimised the identi-
fication of individual cases and the names used to refer to survivors are
not their real names.

THE FAMILIES

The seven families chosen for this study were those where a family
member committed a homicide–suicide, following an apparent dispute
in relation to custody of and/or access to children. To the outside
observer these families seemed to resemble hundreds of other families
where the parents have separated. However, I believe the information
gained from survivors indicates that signs of danger and risk were very
evident in the circumstances preceding the offence, and in some cases
the risk was apparent for years prior to the offence. These factors were
particularly noticeable when the female partner tried to leave the relationship, as several reported trying to do many times before the final
separation. It seems that many in the community knew that risk, in the
form of threats to harm, existed, but no action was taken. Thus, not
only did the man escape accountability for his threats but also, by not
coming to the notice of authorities, he was denied the opportunity to

be referred to an appropriate service that might have helped him to change his behaviour.

A recent study of Australian family homicide showed that 'a quarter of the intimate partner homicides occurred between separated, or divorced couples'. It also found that the incidence of filicide, 'where the child is killed by one parent as a consequence of the actual or pending separation from the other parent', is 9 per cent (Mouzos and Rushforth 2003: 1–2).

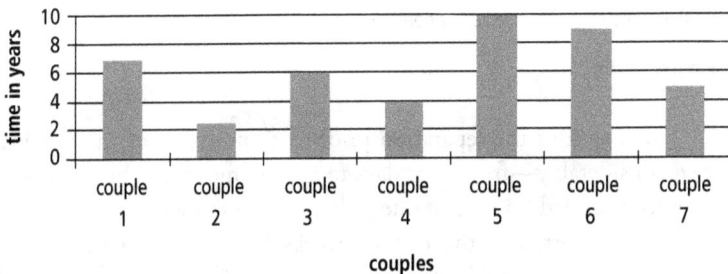

FIGURE 5: Length of marriage or cohabitation

Source: Johnson (2002)

In the seven cases studied, six of the couples had been legally married and the other couple had been in a de facto relationship. The length of the couples' relationships varied (Figure 5). The marriages ranged from four to ten years' duration, although some of the relationships had lasted much longer as the couples had earlier lived as de facto partners. The only de facto relationship in the study had lasted for about two and a half years, although the partners disagreed about its duration and the date of separation, the woman claiming the relationship had finished somewhat earlier than the man acknowledged. It is possible this dispute was related to his initial refusal to accept her separation from him.

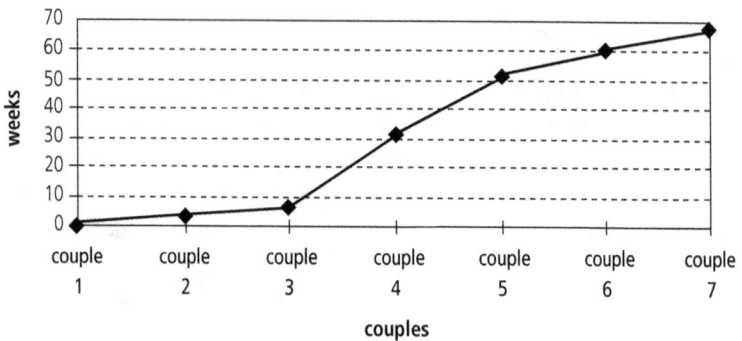

FIGURE 6: Time elapsed since separation

Source: Johnson (2002)

The length of the separation prior to commission of the offence varied considerably—from four days to sixteen months. Three couples had been separated for at least one year. Figure 6 shows that one cluster of offences occurred in the first six weeks following separation, and a second cluster occurred after separation of at least one year. This is consistent with research by Hore and her colleagues, which found the peak danger times for women at risk of homicide by their partners were less than three months after separation, and over a year later (Hore, Gibson and Bordow 1996).

Ages and Occupations

There was a noticeable difference in the age range of the male and female partners: the men were aged between twenty-seven and thirty-nine years, the women between twenty-four and twenty-nine years. The age of the female partner in two couples was unknown.

In every case where the age of the woman was known, the man was older (Figure 7), the difference varying between two and twelve years. In three cases the men were older by five years or more, which gives rise to questions about the male selecting a younger partner whom he may more easily control. Tom had pretended to be younger than he was when he first met Clare. She said: 'He was eleven years older than me.

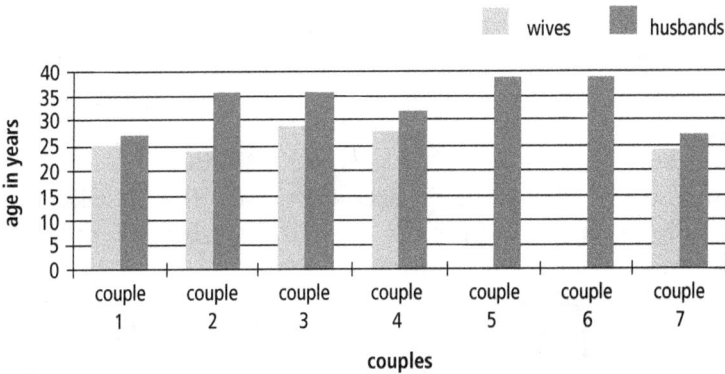

FIGURE 7: Age difference between partners

Source: Johnson (2002)

When I first met him he lied about his age, lied about his name.
I thought it was queer to lie about his name.'

It was not possible to ascertain the occupations of all the couples.
Among the fathers there were two truck drivers, one groundsman, one
computer programmer, one farmer, one invalid pensioner, and one
whose occupation was unknown. Among the mothers there was one
barmaid, one market gardener, three women involved in child-rearing
and home duties, and two whose occupations were unknown. Both of
the women in paid employment outside the home combined this work
with home duties and child-care. One of them was a part-owner in the
business where she worked.

History of the Relationship

Five of the seven relationships were characterised by long-standing un-
happiness and discord, but information about the quality of the other
two relationships could not be located. Where the instigator of the
separation was known, it had been the wife, and in each case it appeared
she had difficulty in getting her partner to accept the separation.

Some women reported having tried to leave previously, but finding this very difficult due to a range of factors which included pregnancy,

fear of violence and family pressure. Narelle recalled: 'Michael's dad would say, "Leave him". My mum would encourage me to work at it, to go back, and to keep trying. She wanted me to have a good marriage and a nice home.'

Ruth described how she had wanted her husband to leave the house when she realised the relationship was over, but it had taken four months to get him to move out. She explained: 'Barry didn't let me separate. He still controlled me.'

All interviewees described the couple's relationship as being characterised by male dominance and control, and all the men were described as being possessive in their relationships both with their partners and with their children. Each person interviewed reported being well aware that the man would not tolerate his partner leaving him, even though in several cases it was reported that the man had been involved with other women prior to the separation.

History of Domestic Violence

It was not known, before I undertook the study, to what extent domestic violence was a previous factor in the spousal relationship. Police offence reports do not contain historical information, as they refer to the offence circumstances only and are of necessity very brief. The Family Court records had minimal information pertaining to the history of violence in some cases, and no record of it at all in others. This is consistent with the findings of Hore, Gibson and Bordow (1996) in their research on the Family Court of Australia.

It is clear from my study that decision-makers in community agencies such as the police and the courts had insufficient documented information about previous threats to harm, and the history of actual violence. In part this may have been a result of under-reporting of domestic violence by respondents, but violence was generally under-recognised by the agencies even when there were clear signs it existed. Some responsibility must be taken by agencies who routinely deal with these issues to ensure their staff have the capacity to elicit information about violence from those who may be traumatised by it, and may be consequently manifesting symptoms such as denial and minimisation.

Women in this study under-reported their partner's violence towards themselves and their children to the Family Court, and the effect on children who witnessed violence was also under-reported or minimised. Where information was provided, the authorities gave it insufficient weight and did not see it in its full context. This is a common occurrence at all levels of society, where 'the crime figures greatly under-estimate the extent of domestic violence, as it is the most under-reported crime in our society, and even when it is reported, it frequently remains un-documented' (Women's Coalition Against Family Violence 1994: 2). Recognition of long-term effects on the emotional well-being of children who witness violence is relatively recent.

It was also apparent from the reports of most participants that the Court of Petty Sessions did not always respond adequately to women making applications for Violence Restraining Orders. One woman reported that her application was dismissed because her husband's solicitor was able to convince the magistrate that the man would change his behaviour, even though he had a long history of stalking and was not attending any counselling or treatment program to help him to cope with the emotional effects of the separation. Even successful applications did not appear to help the women a great deal as the police seemed, to them, to be reluctant to act upon them. When one man was found in his wife's roof, he was not charged with breaching the Restraining Order.

Police responses to complaints of stalking and other threats and harassment from women's ex-partners were inadequate. The police seemed to lack both an understanding of the risks involved, and sufficient appropriate strategies to deal with this type of complaint. In one case, although the woman was assured her name was in the 'drive-by' book (on the route for regular police patrols), she found out afterwards this was not true and her complaints of her husband's stalking had elicited no response.

A 1986 report commissioned by the Western Australian Government stated that police were viewing threats and actual violence as 'domestic' even when couples had been separated for a number of years. At this time a variety of women's complaints surfaced, including:

- Police ignored me/supported my partner.
- Police said it was domestic and there was no Restraining Order upon which to act.
- Police did nothing.
- Police did not seem to want involvement.
- Police suggested I leave home.
- Police did not respond or took too long to respond.

The report recommended that 'Police must recognise and respond to the fact that violence inflicted on an ex-partner is clearly an offence requiring law enforcement' (Western Australian Government 1986: 115). That study, like this one, shows clearly that domestic violence is under-reported and where it is reported the response is ineffective.

In my study, each person interviewed reported at least one form of behaviour in the perpetrator that would be considered as meeting the criteria for domestic violence, including financial, social, emotional, and verbal abuse, as well as extreme acts of violence and sexual abuse. In most cases it was clear there had been a history of various forms of domestic violence in the relationship, which was often minimised by the wife. Respondents also reported the existence of violence or excessive control, as well as possible indications of pathology, in the perpetrator's family of origin.

Some women reported initially that their partner had not been violent, but during the course of the interview disclosed that he had, in fact, engaged in a variety of abusive behaviour. It seemed that women did not necessarily view breaking objects, smashing furniture or the destruction of personal property as acts of violence. Similarly, they did not always see making threats, stalking, and breaking into their homes as violence. For example, Clare denied her ex-partner Tom had been violent towards her. She said: 'There was no violence, no. Control? He liked his own way! He made all the decisions.' She continued: 'He wasn't usually violent to me. He used to smash other things, not me. He used to smash mirrors, vases, a wardrobe.' She described how he restricted her movements and her social contact, including contact with family: 'If I wanted to see my mum I couldn't pack, I had to get out before he could stop me from going. I didn't think at the time it was control.'

An aunt of two of the murdered children said of the couple's relationship that 'it didn't feel right. She always gave in to him. He was a control freak. He always had violence on the brain.'

One woman denied that her husband was physically violent, although she had witnessed his violence towards others. She said: 'He used more mental violence towards me'. Another related a situation of extreme financial abuse where she was not able to make even the most mundane of purchases without her husband's approval:

> When I had my son, I had to fight with my husband to get money. When we went to the supermarket he would query what I was putting in the trolley. Once he threw a can at me in the supermarket. It was embarrassing, an older woman saw it. He had all of our money and I had none.

At the first opportunity he sold her car and used the money to buy himself a four-wheel-drive vehicle. By doing so he ensured she lost the independence of having her own transport and, as her family lived in the country, made it even more difficult for her to leave him.

Clare described her ex-husband Tom as being very secretive.

> He had a post office box, where the mail was delivered to and I was not allowed to open it. We were together two and a half years. I had my daughter and was pregnant with my son when I moved into a unit to get away from him. He would argue or pick fights with my friends and family. For instance, when my nanna came to stay, supposedly for a week, she only stayed one day because he made her cry, he purposely fought with her to make her leave.

Thus over a period of time she became more and more isolated from her family as a result of his behaviour. Tom also reportedly had a locked study, equipped with a steel door, in the couple's home. Clare was never allowed access to this room and he kept the key with him at all times, even when asleep.

Compounding the problems of violence and control that the women experienced, there were reports of obsessive and irrational jealousy. Clare only found out after the offence, when she finally gained access to his study, the extent of Tom's jealousy: 'He went through photograph albums and ripped up pictures of happy times I had had with his cousin and my old boyfriends. I didn't know he'd done this, because he kept them all locked up in his study.'

Women reported that the picture of control and abuse was clearer to them in hindsight. For example Clare, although initially denying that her husband was violent towards her, acknowledged as the interview progressed that there were other forms of abuse in the relationship. She said: 'There were put-downs. He was definitely psychologically abusive. He was a control freak. He made sure who I was with, where I was going. He checked on my movements every day.' She went on to explain how Tom would check the reading on her car's odometer when he returned from work, so that he could ensure she was telling the truth about her movements. She realised that 'he engineered my social isolation'.

In general, there was no recognition among respondents of the long-term effect that witnessing violent behaviour and/or being subjected to other types of abuse had on them.

In some cases violence did not occur only within the spousal relationship. Looking back prior to their marriage, Narelle became aware that, quite early in her relationship, her husband's violence towards another young man had caused her to realise the possible consequences should she decide to leave him for another man. She said:

> When I was seventeen, a year after we started going out, another boy wanted me to go out. Michael found him and broke his nose. Now, when I think about it, I thought to myself then 'I can never go out with anyone else, because he will kill them'.

One woman remembered observing several attempts by the perpetrator to seriously hurt or even kill his adult siblings.

I've seen him throw tools, hammers [at his brothers]. Once he pushed his brother into a silo of wheat and closed the door. He tried to kill him! His intent was to kill him! He was very jealous of his older brother and his brother was very jealous of him.

Danni reported that her sister's husband had a long history of violence:

I saw what he was like. He had a big fight with his brother over money once. He was weird. It was because he couldn't get his own way. He did nothing that day, but the next day he took a gun and went looking for his brother to kill him. He intended to kill him. Luckily, he couldn't find him.

Clare reported that Tom's violence and possessiveness had caused her to lose her job. She explained:

We had a work dinner. When it was time to leave the boss went round and kissed all the women on the cheek. Tom was furious, he was going to punch my boss, it was embarrassing, the men had their jackets off in the car park ready to fight. Tom went off, like a madman, in the car on the way home. I should have got out then! The next day the boss called me in and sacked me. He told me I should leave my husband.

She added:

Tom was very controlling. He kept me from seeing my family. If my mum drove all the way to Perth, he would not make her welcome. He was arrogant and rude. He acted like he thought he was someone special. He used to work out at the gym a lot. He didn't have any friends except one.

Some years before killing the two children from his marriage, his stepson and himself, Peter had been in a previous (de facto) relationship. When his partner had tried to leave him, Peter had reportedly tried to ram her head into a kitchen counter while she was holding their baby, attempted to choke her, had pulled out a lump of her hair and grabbed her by the throat. Peter had illegally taken his infant child from that relationship and refused to return him to his mother who had legal custody. This woman needed to seek a court order to have the child, then aged twelve months, returned to her care. The details of this did not appear to have been available to court officials when they were considering this man's circumstances and the possible risk to his subsequent children at the time of his break-up with Rita, his second wife.

There were instances of male partners demonstrating selfishness and disregard for the welfare of their partner or children. The women appeared to be powerless in the face of this behaviour. One explained, 'I had to sleep on the floor when I was five months pregnant, so he could get a good sleep in bed'. She went on to describe another incident where she had been enjoying rare social contact with members of her husband's family: 'Once his cousins were visiting. We were looking at photos. Because I was having a nice time, he went and woke our daughter up so I would have to attend to her.'

One woman described a long-term plan she had made to escape from the restrictive and abusive relationship she felt trapped in. She had eventually managed to return to her home town, where she had family support, but her husband resigned from his job and followed her, a distance of several hundred kilometres. She said:

> After I had got rid of him I came home, but he followed. One night I was with friends out dancing. He wanted to have the kids to baby-sit them. It was late at night and I was dancing with a man, but he came up to where I was and abused me. He had left one child alone in the car, and brought the other with him, on his hip.

Elliott and Shanahan reported that perpetrators of domestic violence 'do not realise that their behaviour constitutes domestic violence, wife assault or wife bashing, and, they do not register that their behaviour could be "criminal"; it is normal (and justifiable) to them' (1988: 3). Men interviewed in their study reported that they believed if a woman wanted to leave the relationship they were justified in using force to prevent her. This view was based on an 'overwhelming sense of self-righteousness' which caused them to feel that 'the use of violence was necessary to force upon their wives their point of view', so that if 'the man wants a woman to stay, he feels he can use violence or he feels he can use his strength to keep his family together' (Elliott and Shanahan 1988: 8).

In considering the information pertaining to domestic violence against the women in these cases, it is worth noting that one study on domestic violence found that where there were children, in 21 per cent of cases the man had also assaulted them. It also found that in 56 per cent of cases the children had witnessed their mother being attacked, and in 11 per cent the children had intervened physically in the violence between their parents (Johnson, Ross and Vinson, cited in O'Donnell and Craney 1982: 42).

History of Substance Abuse by the Perpetrator

There were some indications that the perpetrators had abused alcohol and drugs. One man was described as a binge drinker who would sometimes leave his young family for days while he engaged in heavy drinking bouts with his friends, and in two cases the man was reported to use cannabis but to what extent could not be determined. In the other cases, there was no information about substance abuse. However, Ewing reports that

> alcohol abuse, mental illness, and criminality also bear strong statistical relationships to intra-familial homicide. Among intra-familial killings examined by the Justice Department, nearly half the perpetrators and roughly a third of the victims had been drinking at the time of the killing (1997: 10).

This is confirmed by another study: 'Alcohol and drug use is known to be a factor in over 30 per cent of spousal homicides, and in 60 per cent of cases of domestic violence' (Johnson, Ross and Vinson, cited in O'Donnell and Craney 1982: 34). In Easteal's study of Australian

spousal homicide, 65 per cent of non-Aboriginal Australian-born offenders consumed alcohol at the time of the offence, and the figure was
89 per cent for Aboriginal offenders (1993: 81). Another researcher says
'the use of various substances such as alcohol or illegal or prescription
drugs is a common problem amongst filicide offenders' (Crimmins et
al. 1997, cited in Wilczynski 1997: 84). Even though my research did
not identify substance abuse as a contributing factor in familicide, the
weight of evidence indicates that it is a factor in filicide, spousal and
other intra-familial homicide. More research is required.

History of Mental Disorder in the Perpetrator

Mouzos found the incidence of mental disorder among homicide
offenders varies tremendously between countries, from 2 per cent in Sri
Lanka to 53 per cent in northern Sweden (1999b: 2). However, it is
difficult to compare these figures accurately due to variations in diagnostic criteria between countries. Moreover, the time frames, sample
sizes, and methodologies also varied significantly. Mouzos discovered in
her nine-year study that, in Australia, the incidence of mental disorder
in homicide offenders appears to be lower than that of the general
population. However, she recommended caution in accepting this
because the data was obtained exclusively from police offence reports
and depended on the perpetrator showing signs of mental disorder at
the time of the homicide (1999b: 2–5).

Police offence reports are brief and, by definition, are compiled by
individuals not trained in the assessment of psychiatric conditions or
mental disorders. Obviously, in the case of murder–suicide the perpetrator's death prevents an accurate determination about their mental
health at the time of the offence, or when the bodies were found.
In these cases, reports collected subsequently about the individual's
emotional state and behaviour leading up to the offence provide more
useful information about mental health. Such information cannot
change the outcome of offences already committed, but it may help to
provide guidelines for preventing future offences. As Ewing notes:

> Far from all family killers suffer from diagnosable mental illness.
> And not all who do ever come to the attention of a professional

who could make that diagnosis. Still, many individuals who kill family members are not only mentally ill but have sought mental health treatment prior to the killing or are in such treatment at the time of the killing. As a result mental health professionals are often in a position to predict and possibly prevent lethal family violence (1997: 157).

In my study it was difficult to establish whether the perpetrator had a history of mental disorder, not only because the offence reports lacked detail, but also because there were no psychiatric or psychological reports or assessments. Even where a Family Court file recorded disturbances in the behaviour of the perpetrator that may have indicated mental disorder, I had no means to establish whether or not this was the case.

There were, however, some extreme examples of disturbed behaviour. For example, one man frequently slept outside his ex-partner's house wrapped in a sheet of plastic to protect himself from the rain. This man had previously been fastidious in his appearance and attire, but now appeared scruffy, bearded and dishevelled. One young woman whose daughter was murdered described her husband's obsessiveness: 'He kept a record of all telephone calls. He was so meticulous. He made lists at night of what he had to do the next day. He used to phone me every day to check on my whereabouts.'

One relative spoke of the maternal family's attachment to the perpetrator. She said: 'We were friends. We liked him.' She described how she and others in the family would try to provide emotional support when he was depressed as he had refused to seek professional support. Another reported that, although the perpetrator had shown signs of bizarre behaviour prior to the offence, as far as she knew he had no psychiatric history.

Understandably, due to the separation, and in most cases the resulting alienation between the parties, the women generally did not know whether their ex-partners had been diagnosed or were receiving treatment for any disorder. In one case, though, a woman reported that she knew that her husband had been prescribed anti-depressant medication, which he combined with excessive amounts of alcohol.

It is evident there were disturbances in the behaviour of most of the perpetrators leading up to the offences, some of which only came to light later. Most women noticed some indication of what they thought was depression, which in some cases had been evident for some months, and in others a recurring problem for years. Furthermore, all respondents described dysfunctional dynamics in the families of the offenders. One remarked: 'His family was queer. You had to make an appointment to see them. When I met him he hated his dad for how his dad treated his mum. I told him, "Your dad is old, you have to have a relationship with him".'

Narelle had married into a wealthy farming family. She found her mother-in-law to be very controlling:

Michael's mother would tell me how to dress, what to wear to town, who to look at, who not to look at, when we went to town. Everyone called her 'the queen'. She would say, 'I'll give you lessons'. She taught me not to smile. She said I smiled too much at people who were poor. She told me who I could smile at and who I was not allowed to smile at. I was young, I didn't know any different, I smiled at everyone.

One woman described her husband as having come from a very disturbed family background: 'His family dynamics are very interesting. It is pathological, psychotic. There was a history of undiagnosed mental illness in the family. They were controlling and possessive, there was conditional love and physical abuse.' A relative from another family described the perpetrator's family as being very strange and closed to outside influence. She said: 'He was too close to his mother. They did everything together except have sex.'

So, although the respondents did not state that the offenders had been diagnosed with a psychiatric illness, their descriptions of the offenders' behaviour throughout the relationship and leading up to the offence, the reported family dynamics, and the offences themselves, raise questions about the presence of such an illness. It seems likely that depression or some sort of personality disorder, in particular borderline personality disorder, caused the offenders' erratic behaviour following separation. Again, the possible existence of mental disturbance in the perpetrators cries out for further research.

History of Sexual Abuse

Sexual abuse is another area requiring further exploration. It is accepted that sexual abuse is common in violent intimate relationships, and many women report that incidents of domestic violence culminate in coercive sexual acts and even rape.

Currently, there is limited research about its existence in relationships where separation has precipitated lethal violence against children followed by perpetrator suicide. When asked if there had been a history of sexual abuse in the relationship, most respondents initially answered no. But it often became clear as the interview progressed that there were indications of sexual deviance or sexual violence on the part of the perpetrator, usually associated with his need to control the victim.

When one woman was asked about the existence of sexual abuse in her relationship with her long-term de facto partner, who was ten years her senior, she replied: 'No, not really. I wouldn't have sex with him because he was such an arsehole. I busted him on phone sex once.' This woman believed her partner was engaged in some kind of deviant sexual behaviour, but was never able to confirm this.

Danni reported that after separation the perpetrator had changed: 'He turned weird sexually. He wanted anal sex after separation.' Another respondent said: 'He would fit a broad definition of being sexually violent. He was into pornography. He would sit up and watch it, then demand sex when I got home. If I refused he would accuse me of having affairs.'

From the evidence presented by survivors, it seems that sexual violence usually targeted the woman and was associated with an obsessive need by the perpetrator to control his partner. However, there is one important exception to this. It raises significant issues about the knowledge required by judicial officers in the Family Court to make sound, child-focused judgements.

In this case, there were serious allegations that the father had sexually abused all three children. One, the only girl in the family, had suffered from recurrent vaginal infections for years. In spite of a recommendation by Princess Margaret Hospital for Children that contact with the father cease until the allegations had been dealt with, the Family Court ordered unsupervised contact. The children's mother defied the Court Order and denied contact. The little girl's recurrent infection cleared up quickly and did not recur. It is not clear from the documents I studied why contact was ordered, but it appears the Family Court saw both parties as being unnecessarily derogatory towards one another. Due to lack of experience and knowledge, the court and the other agencies involved did not coordinate their responses to ensure the children's safety. It is not clear whether the court was fully aware of previous threats made by the perpetrator to harm the children. From the information available, a professional trained in the social sciences would have had serious concerns about the children's safety, but it is doubtful that a legally trained person would assess the risk in the same way (see recommendations in Chapter 8). These children were murdered during a court-ordered, unsupervised access visit.

Criminal History

Frequently, perpetrators of spousal violence are reported to have a history of driving offences and violence. O'Donnell and Craney found that more that 40 per cent of attackers had previous convictions (1982: 38). At this time, it is not known to what extent perpetrators of familicide resemble perpetrators of other forms of spousal violence in relation to criminal history. This also requires further study, especially to develop screening and assessment tools.

THE CHILDREN

Within these seven families there were sixteen children living with their parents prior to their parents' separation. All except one were the biological children of both parents. This child was the stepson of the perpetrator, but had been brought up by this man since the age of eight months.

The children in the families were all young, ranging in age from seventeen months to eight years. Eight were boys and eight were girls.

The boy who survived was eighteen months old at the time of the offence.

SUMMARY

In six of the seven families studied, the couples were legally married and aged between twenty-four and thirty-nine years of age. They had been together for between two-and-a-half and ten years. The families had between one and three children each, aged between seventeen months and eight years of age. Time elapsed between separation and familicide varied from four days to sixteen months.

It is clear that domestic violence, in all its variants, was a significant factor in the five cases where details of the relationship between the spouses could be ascertained. It was reported that children had witnessed some of the violence but it is not clear to what extent this was the case. Although sexual abuse in the marital relationship certainly occurred in some cases, its extent could not be fully determined. In one family there was strong evidence of child sexual abuse. Some of the reported behaviours of perpetrators indicate the possibility of substance abuse, or mental illness or both, but again it was not possible to verify this. Finally, there were indications of deterioration in the mental health of some of the perpetrators in events leading up to the offence. As before, this could not be confirmed, and is worthy of further study.

The Break-up

In Family Court counselling, and in separation counselling generally, it is common to find that men complain that their partner's departure has been a sudden shock, whereas the wife reports a long history of dissatisfaction with the relationship, which she has tried to address. Often a woman says that she had asked her partner to attend counselling when problems first arose in their relationship, only to be told he saw nothing wrong. Women reported being told by their partner: 'If you have a problem you go to counselling, I don't have any problems'. Many men agree to go to counselling only after the wife views the relationship as irreparable. By this time women have already attended counselling, have moved on from their partner, feel clearer about what they want in a relationship, and are more independent as a result.

In all cases researched here, the survivors described the break-up of the couple's relationship as extremely difficult. Each reported that the perpetrator was reluctant to let his partner go. Each of the women had tried to leave the relationship many times before she finally succeeded. In almost every case her attempts to leave the relationship had spanned years. Each woman described the last attempt as being characterised by a firm resolve, on her part, that this would be the final separation. It is interesting to speculate to what extent their steadfast resolve communicated itself to the perpetrator, and to what extent he may have realised there would be no turning back this time, regardless of the woman's previous history of leaving and then returning.

Survivors were asked to describe the couple's relationship prior to separation and the circumstances leading up to it. All described a long-term deterioration in the relationship. Ruth explained how the deterioration of her relationship had spanned years. 'It was a breakdown of communication. He withdrew totally. He changed the day our first child was born. He never talked. After the second child was born there was a slight improvement but this was short term, then he got worse.'

Narelle had persevered with her marriage in the belief that the problems could be resolved, but finally, she determined she could not remain in the marriage unless there were some major changes in her husband's behaviour.

> It was near Christmas and I just wanted to be happy for Christmas. So I made a decision and gave him an ultimatum. I said I wanted him to give up the football coaching and the drinking, and then I went away with the children. Later, we spoke together and talked about him buying a house in town, so he could see the children when he wanted to. I had left before, when I was pregnant with my first child, I had gone and stayed with my mum for a week. Then, when I found out I was pregnant, I went back.

Clare had also made several attempts to leave her husband but had found this very difficult.

> When I left the first time, he kept hanging around all the time. I knew I had to get smarter. I knew I had to get back to my home town, to be with my family. One day I told him I was going to leave and go home. That's when he got really violent.

Later, Clare reported finding herself with an unplanned pregnancy, 'I was stupid enough to sleep with him. I'm so angry with myself for staying.' She realised another child would tie her into the abusive relationship for an even longer period, and therefore made the painful decision to have an abortion. She described this decision as being based on the future welfare of her two existing children, as she did not want them to grow up within her abusive relationship with their father. Her feelings of desperation at the time were evident, as she related what had happened:

> I had to get rid of the baby, or I'd never have got away, I had to do the ultimate. He drove me to the appointment for the abortion and fought with me all the way. My mum was angry about the abortion too, but I knew I would never get away from him with three children. I never slept with him afterwards, I could never get sucked in again.

After the abortion Clare planned her escape carefully. Eventually she was able to return with her children to the country, where she could receive support from her family. Clare said she had needed to be very calculating and patient in order to escape from Tom: She said: 'I hated him. I knew I couldn't get away straight away. I knew I had to bide my time. He always knew where I'd been because of checking the kilometres on the car.'

Narelle explained there had been problems in her marriage for some time:

> It had been going on for two years. We lived out of town and I only went to the grocery shop once a week. He was involved in football and he coached twice a week. When he went into town to coach, he wouldn't come home. He'd stay in town for three nights and go out drinking with his mates. I was left to feed the pigs and to do all the farm work, and I had two children to look after. I complained about him not coming home, so I came to Perth and stayed with my grandma. He came down to see me and he had love bites all over his neck. He explained it by saying the boys had pinned him down in the pub and done it to him.

Afterwards, Narelle discovered Michael had been involved with a number of other women throughout their relationship.

An aunt of two of the murdered children confirmed that the wife had tried to leave before:

> He was losing power. He was gentle until he couldn't get his own way. He was obsessed with her and would never let her go, although she tried to get away. Once she left him and moved into an upstairs unit. He came to the place where she was staying and climbed up the side of the house like a spider, he started to smash the window to break in and so she let him in. That's when I saw the cracks in his personality. He said he would never let her or the kids go. So she returned.

Ruth had tried to encourage her ex-husband to see the children regularly but he complained that he found this hard to do. She recalled: 'He never used to take the children anywhere. He would come to my house for contact because he couldn't cope with them. He would never come for a child [for contact] if they were sick.'

One woman reported a deterioration in the relationship with her husband that went back to the birth of their first child and which may have indicated an irrational jealousy.

> He was obsessive prior to the separation and there were some instances of this when we were courting. It was escalating. After our first child was born he said, 'I've lost part of you to the baby'. The baby cried a lot and he was jealous of the child. He used to say, 'Shut that fucking kid up'.

Ruth described how her husband would entreat her to resume their relationship: 'He would tower over me, harangue me for hours, saying, "You will take me back". It's so hard to say No. You get worn down.'

Several women felt pressured to stay in the relationship by members of their own family as well as by their husband's. One said, 'His mum offered me a house and a car to go back. She offered me money. I didn't take it.'

Another respondent described how, before the offence, she had felt her husband had at last accepted the separation, that he was reconciled to the fact there would be no reunification. At first, somewhat perversely, he had wanted her to refuse him the divorce, which he had initiated, and had begged her to fight the action in the court and tell the magistrate hearing the case she did not want the marriage to end. She had refused to fight the divorce because she was fearful of doing anything that might encourage his stalking behaviour.

In every case where it could be determined, the wife initiated the separation. This is not surprising because wives initiate the majority of all separations. It appeared most had attempted to leave previously but had been prevented, either by the reaction of their partner, or by their fear of how he might react.

The Family Court

As far as I could find out from the documents and interviews, five of the seven couples had no current application before the Family Court at the time of the offence. Of these five, two couples had never used the court process in any capacity. One of these couples had been separated for only four days, so if there had been a dispute it was of brief duration, while the other had been separated for a year. A third couple had not appeared before the court, but had simply used the court registry to file a Deed of Agreement (which would indicate, superficially at least, that there was no dispute about children's matters).

A fourth couple were awaiting the Decree Absolute (the final order for divorce issued by the court which allows the parties to remarry) which would have been issued in three months, and this would have completed the court process. A Decree Nisi (the provisional order for divorce granted by the court, which becomes absolute unless cause is shown to the contrary) had been issued five days before the offence. It appeared from the court records there had never been a serious dispute about access in this case, other than that the mother wanted the children's access with their father to be regular and predictable, for the sake of the children, but the husband had claimed not to be able to be consistent with access, as he found it too personally distressing. As a result there had been large gaps in his access visits with his children.

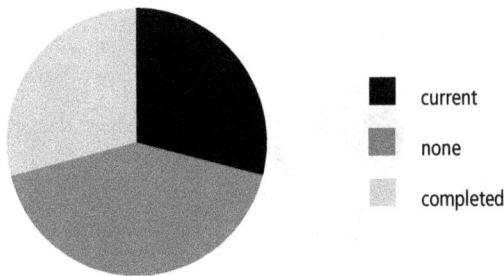

current

completed

FIGURE 8: Existence of court dispute

Source: Johnson (2002)

A fifth couple had made a legal agreement about custody and access using a Minute of Consent Orders. A full trial and a judgement of the court had resolved another case, although this was to be reviewed.

Based on this information, one could reasonably conclude that only two of these cases had a current dispute in relation to custody and access at the time of the offence. However, this conclusion may not be accurate, given the complex set of circumstances in every case. It is far more likely that, in at least three cases, one of the parties was not satisfied with the outcome. In those cases where consent had apparently been reached (whether or not as part of the court process), it could be argued that both parties had not necessarily agreed to arrangements regarding the children. Certainly, in the interviews, it became apparent that some of the women had felt pressured to make an agreement they were not really satisfied with. It may have been that the men were no more satisfied with the Consent Order than the women were.

In looking at the outcomes of the court process, one needs to understand how litigants may experience pressures from different sources and for different reasons. Firstly, the majority of people who separate do not use the Family Court to determine custody and access, preferring to make their own arrangements with respect to the children. Others simply use it to register a Deed of Agreement, or a Minute of Consent Orders, either of which they may draw up on their own or with the help of a solicitor. Either way, this does not require their attendance in a

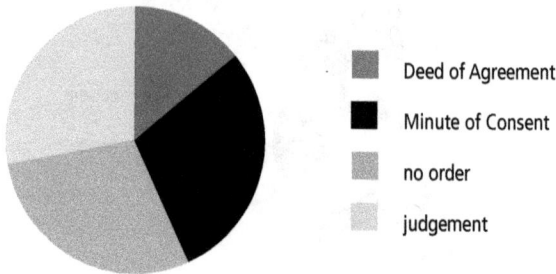

Deed of Agreement

Minute of Consent

no order

judgement

FIGURE 9: Type of court order

Source: Johnson (2002)

courtroom or at court counselling. Secondly, it is not always possible to effectively resolve the dispute, even when a Consent Order is achieved through counselling and/or the court process, because consent is often perceived by one or both parties as having been coerced. The 'agreement' thus reached may be a risk to the safety of the children where there has been prior abuse, or where there are current concerns for the children's well-being as a result of their father's response to separation.

When individuals seek court orders or file an application seeking court counselling in relation to custody or access, this in itself indicates some level of dispute between the parties. The Family Court aims to achieve agreement, thus preventing a lengthy and costly trial. Consequently, parties often report feeling coerced into agreements that they do not feel wholly satisfied with. In relationships where there is a power imbalance, the more vulnerable person will often acquiesce to the stronger partner. In addition, the considerable expense of litigation causes some parties to make agreements that they do not believe are in the best interests of either their children or themselves, because they see their legal costs spiralling and the chances of obtaining the outcome they want diminishing. In each of the three cases in this study that were scheduled to return to court, the children were murdered and the man committed suicide before this could occur.

It is worth noting that many couples involved in bitter disputes concerning their children do not avail themselves of the court process.

Reasons for this vary. For Aboriginal and Torres Strait Islanders, who generally do not seem to use the Family Court, the reason may be cultural. In the case of low income earners, it may be financial, as not all low income earners are eligible for legal aid and hiring a solicitor is not often economically possible. Even though the Family Court encourages people to represent themselves, many who might benefit from this option do not have the necessary confidence or literacy skills. In the case of women who have suffered long-term abuse from their partners, it is a well observed phenomenon in the Family Court that the ordeal of having to face the perpetrator, in an adversarial courtroom scenario, precludes this as an option, even if they have achieved some level of recovery and improved self-esteem since separation.

The pertinent question is: how are orders consented to in cases where there is obviously a significant dispute between the parties about custody or access, and where one or both parties believe their children to be at risk during contact with the other parent? The answer is that parties often feel pressured by their lawyers, by members of the judiciary or by the court process itself, to reach agreement, as it is accepted that only in very exceptional cases will parents be denied unsupervised access with their children. Even where supervised access is initially ordered it is often understood that, if no problems are visible in the parent–child relationship after several supervised sessions, further access will be unsupervised. This may be a reasonable expectation, but in cases where there is child abuse—particularly sexual abuse—appearances may be deceptive. The parent–child relationship may appear satisfactory at the supervised access centre, but the observers witness the interaction for a relatively short period in a closed, controlled environment. In many cases the observers are students with limited knowledge of child abuse and child trauma.

It is exceedingly difficult for members of the judiciary to decide whether access should be supervised or not. Behaviour described in affidavits and other reports may clearly indicate to the trained reader that a child is at risk, but those who lack training in the areas of family dynamics, domestic violence and child abuse may not see the signs of danger, even though they have extensive legal training.

In addition, in my experience, women who have suffered years of abuse, or whose children have disclosed abuse, understandably appear emotional and/or ambivalent about these issues when facing their lawyers or the court. Unfortunately, depending on how she expresses this emotion, the woman's credibility and thus the veracity of the allegations can be called into question. Women described their feelings of powerlessness, frustration and confusion while involved in the court process at the Court of Petty Sessions and the Family Court. They reported that judicial officers were naive about domestic violence and about the perpetrator's ability to manipulate lawyers and the court. Some men refused to sign legal papers as a way of stalling the court process, and denied stalking behaviour knowing there were no witnesses other than their ex-wives. Women found that where there were witnesses, they were easily intimidated, and did not generally wish to appear in court.

Ruth explained how, even though her husband had initiated the divorce he would not sign a Deed of Agreement prepared by her, so an application for a Minute of Consent Orders had to be filed.

It was an application for divorce. Divorce initiated by my husband. We used the court registry for a Minute of Consent Orders. I had lodged a Deed of Agreement but he wouldn't sign the typed copy. I took out a Restraining Order for myself and for the children. He couldn't have access until he drew up the papers. Court was finished apart from Decree Absolute. We used the court process for a Minute of Consent and for the divorce.

Clare reported feeling pressured by her lawyer to agree to contact but she agreed to supervised contact and signed a Minute of Consent. It was clear in the interview that she believed this was the end of the court proceedings, as far as she knew. She said, 'Court was finished. Open and shut. Next please!' However, the court records clearly showed this was only an interim order and that the couple had been expected to return to counselling and to the court. This shows that litigants may not fully understand the court process, especially in cases where they are under extreme stress, and this may influence their behaviour in relation to their seeking of orders or their signing of agreements.

Of the four cases that had appeared in the Family Court, all had attended Family Court counselling in accordance with the relevant Acts which require counselling before a court hearing. In one of these, a further counselling appointment had been arranged, but was never kept due to the offence. In another, as mentioned earlier, the court had asked the Counselling Service to report on the effect that the contact had on the children, after a period of access following a judgement of the court.

The four couples who had court counselling to try to resolve the custody or access dispute had attended only one session. Single-session counselling is common at the Family Court, as the service is primarily engaged in assisting couples to reach agreement on custody and access with respect to children. The Counselling Service has not traditionally provided long-term couple counselling as this is not deemed to be its role.

Clare reported being told by her lawyer that she must agree to access even after an incident in which her husband had been late returning the children. Tom had telephoned her in a distressed state and said he was parked in the bush with the children, who could be heard crying in the background. In hindsight, it appeared this had been either a rehearsal or a previous attempt to kill both himself and the children. As a result, Clare saw court counselling as a waste of time. Her lawyer had instructed her as to what agreement she should make concerning access, and she had felt completely powerless in the situation. She asked: 'Why did I have to go to court counselling? Why did I have to be in the same room with him? Tom was so brash and cocky.'

AFTER SEPARATION

Research consistently finds that violence against battered women escalates significantly, often to fatal or potentially fatal proportions, any time these women try to take any control over their lives or the battering relationship (Ewing 1997: 22).

All except one of the women interviewed reported some level of violence during cohabitation, and all indicated there had been violence following attempts to leave the relationship. The violence often occurred in the presence of the children and showed an apparent disregard for the emotional effect this might have on them.

Escalation of Violence After Separation

Men, it has been noted, often start to beat their wives when their wives try to assert themselves in some way or establish some degree of independence (Gelles 1987: 136–41). Consequently, survivors were asked whether they thought the violence had got better or worse since separation. The majority reported it had become worse, but that sometimes the violence took new forms. One woman, who had previously been subjected primarily to economic, social and verbal abuse, was tied up and gagged, then beaten by her partner, when she announced that she was leaving him. Her husband then left the house for several hours, leaving her restrained, with their young child who had witnessed these events, clinging to her in fear. She recounted what had happened:

> When I told him I was leaving, he tied my feet and hands. He pulled my hair and was shaking me. At one stage he had my mouth all tied up. He yelled abuse. Most of the time I wouldn't answer him when he was verbally abusive. Then he'd get angry 'cos I wasn't answering. He was hitting me in front of our daughter. I was screaming, 'Don't let her see it!' He was so cruel! I was crying and crying. She was screaming and screaming. He didn't care, he just pushed her out of the way, he didn't care.

Her distress became more evident as she recalled how powerless she had felt throughout this ordeal, and as she remembered her husband's total disregard for their daughter's fear and anguish. She had been particularly upset because the restraints prevented her using her hands, so she was unable to hold and comfort her daughter after her husband left the house.

Clare was not the only woman who experienced being bound and gagged. Theresa was tied, gagged and assaulted by her husband Murray before he abducted and murdered their two children and then committed suicide. Few details were available about this family, including whether or not the couple's relationship was violent before the separation. However, people on the periphery of the relationship believed that Murray, before abducting the children from school, had threatened to harm them.

Even where physical violence had not been present in the relationship before the separation, the male reacted violently after the separation. Ruth said:

> When I asked him to leave, at the point of separation, it escalated to violence. It was worked out that he would leave and return at a later date to get his belongings. He came back to the house. He screamed and yelled in front of the children. He pinned me to the wall and I threatened to get the police. He threw me at the chest of drawers, in front of the children, I'd never seen him so angry, I was terrified, I'd never seen him like that before.

As we have seen, most women had tried to extricate themselves from the relationship several times, albeit unsuccessfully, before their final separation. Clare noted that on the second occasion she tried to leave, Tom's violence towards her increased. 'He was more violent after the second separation. I told him, "When Christmas is over I'm going, I'm leaving". I was twenty-two when I first left him, twenty-four the second time.'

A relative of one man observed that, although he did not become any more violent than he had been before, he became very introspective and showed signs of extreme possessiveness: 'The violence didn't get worse, but he got more inwards looking. He could never talk about his feelings. He thought they belonged to him, she and the kids belonged to him.'

Interestingly, Narelle, who reported violence increasing when she first left her husband, indicated that just before the offence (when she had made the final decision not to return) Michael seemed to have made some resolve to change: 'It was the opposite [to increased violence]. He was supportive. He wasn't like himself, like a robot, like he'd turned himself into something else.'

This report was inconsistent with others. Given that the offence happened within days of this change in behaviour, it seems possible that Michael, realising the strength of Narelle's resolve not to return, had made up his mind to commit the offence. This seems to be characteristic of many suicides; the person seems to reach a position of acceptance and calm, even including attempts at restitution for past wrongs, before taking their life.

In his study of European suicide, Retterstol noted that 'the pre-suicidal syndrome sometimes includes a calm and serene attitude which can be misinterpreted as an improvement and may only become understandable afterwards' (1993: 138). If in this case Michael's prior intent was to commit suicide, then it follows that the murder of his children may have been due to a lack of individuation, an extension of his own suicide. Alternatively, in light of what was said about his extreme possessiveness, once his mind was set on suicide he was unwilling to leave the children to be brought up by another man.

Another woman, whose relationship had become violent at the point of separation, reported the violence took on a new dimension after separation, which she found terrifying and which totally disrupted her lifestyle. She said, 'The violence got worse, he started stalking'.

Stalking

There were reports of intense and long-term stalking behaviour by the perpetrator after separation. There were even two cases of the perpetrator hiding in the woman's roof and watching her movements through the ceiling. In Clare's case, the police removed Tom from the roof. Because he was dirty and dishevelled, they allowed him to take a shower before they conveyed him to the train station, so that he could leave town. She reported feeling violated; both by his presence in her home, which she had secured for herself and the children after separation, and by the police allowing him to shower in her bathroom.

The couple had been separated for months before this incident and Tom had never lived in this house. Clare recalled being in total shock when the police removed him from the ceiling where he had been observing her. As a result, she did not think to ask the police to charge him, assuming this would be normal procedure. Although subject to a current Restraining Order, Tom was not arrested or charged with breaking and entering, breach of the order or any other offence. Clare believed that if he had been, he could very well have been in jail at the time the offence was ultimately committed. She said:

> If he was a stranger he would have been charged [for being in the roof]. Instead he was escorted out of town. I hate that they didn't charge him. When I asked them why they didn't they said, 'You didn't ask to have him charged'. If he was Joe Bloggs I wouldn't have had to press charges, and anyway, I had a Restraining Order.

Following the offence Clare felt compelled to move house once again.

Clare believes Tom had been in the roof for a week before being detected. Mental health professionals would consider such behaviour very disturbed, but the police not only allowed him to go free without charging him, they also did not arrange any psychiatric assessment or medical treatment. It is likely that police are not adequately trained to identify offenders whose mental health would make them likely to pose a risk to themselves or others.

Ruth too experienced long-term stalking by her ex-husband Barry. He would watch her from his hiding place in the roof of her house, although she was unaware of it at the time. She recalled:

> I caught him stalking soon after [the separation]. He used to drive to where I worked then follow me home. Then when the Consent Order went through he appeared to settle down. I quit work because I couldn't cope and I couldn't sleep. No-one else ever saw him because he was as cunning as a fox, so I couldn't get a witness. I think he was in my roof, I thought at first I had possums, so I rang my dad once to come over at two o'clock in the morning.

Barry used to walk up and down outside the house. The kids would see the shadow. I couldn't sleep at night so I used to sleep in the day, my daughter couldn't sleep either. This one night, I could hear breathing in the passage, I heard puffing and I just froze, I couldn't get out of bed. I made my father stay until 5 am. I always thought I had been stupid, but afterwards Barry confessed to watching me, and he described incidents he had seen but could not hear. He must have been in the ceiling! A tree overhung my roof and he would use this to climb up. I tied fishing line in the tree and he fell over. I think he had also had a key to the house, because he rang my friend's house to speak to the children. It was a silent number, which he could only have obtained from being in my house. I could feel when he was outside, but I got so bloody paranoid, no-one would listen to me.

Reported Deterioration of Mental Health

As previously noted, respondents generally described the perpetrators as having traits in their personality, such as obsessiveness or a need to control, which made them difficult to live with prior to separation. These were major factors in the wife's decision to leave the relationship. As we have seen, the men were usually violent or abusive towards their partners. Most respondents described the perpetrators' mental state and behaviour after separation as deteriorating markedly. No-one reported knowing that the men had been diagnosed with a mental illness— except for one woman who knew that her ex-partner had been prescribed anti-depressants—but all reported depressive symptoms in the perpetrators. It is possible the perpetrators had been diagnosed and were receiving treatment prior to the offence, but this was unknown to the women at the time, and did not become apparent to them even after the offence. Narelle recalled of Michael:

He did get into depressive states. A long time ago, when he got depressed, he wanted to go into the army, he said he just wanted to get away from everything, and from everyone. He used to talk

to my mum, when he felt depressed, because he loved my mother
and she used to try to help him.

Danni read psychology text books extensively after the offence to
try to understand why the incident had happened. She believes, in her
case, that the father of her nephew and niece had had severe emotional
problems over a long period of time. 'He was definitely depressed, and
I mean clinically depressed. He was searching for his identity.' Addi-
tionally, she reported a long-term deterioration in his mental health
before the familicide. 'He got worse. More thinking, more inward,
more controlling. The children's mother knew something wasn't right
for years, but he wouldn't let her leave.'

One source, who reported enjoying a positive relationship with
the perpetrator prior to the offence, said: 'He admitted being depressed
but he couldn't talk about problems in the marriage. He never showed
his feelings. He never saw a psychologist. We used to try to help him by
talking to him.' She said, 'I know he went into depression [after she
left]. He told us. He never saw a counsellor. He would drink or play
sport to lift himself out of it. He got depressed about money.' Ruth's
husband disappeared once. 'He went missing for twenty-four hours.
Then he appeared [as though nothing was wrong] and behaved as
though he thought it was funny. I thought it was very strange behaviour
and I refused to let him back in the house.'

These bizarre changes in the men's behaviour may have been
indicative of a deterioration in their mental health prior to the offence.
The changes were noticed but were not fully understood at the time by
ex-partners, friends or families. They did not understand the signifi-
cance of the altered behaviour, and had no idea where to go for help.

Clare recalled that after the offence a health professional was asked
to comment in the media on both the offence and the events leading up
to it. This person referred to Tom's obsession and made it clear that his
behaviour should have been interpreted as a warning sign.

After finally freeing themselves from years of controlling behaviour,
abuse and violence, some women started to doubt their own mental
health when their ex-husbands began stalking them. Friends and family

members were sceptical of their allegations, leading the women to doubt their own perception of the risk posed to them by their ex-partner. Often the stalking occurred late at night, but when police arrived the man had usually disappeared. The ploys some men used to observe their wife's movements were quite extreme, but there was seldom evidence of this at the time. For example, one woman discovered after the offence that her husband had been booking early morning calls to assist him in his stalking. She recalled: 'When I got his telephone bill [after the offence] I found he was getting wake-up calls for 2 or 3 am so he had time to check on me and then go to work at 5 am'.

Threats of Self-Harm by Perpetrator

Familicide has many of the characteristics of suicide, including prior threats and the leaving of notes (Schneidman 1993: 93). Of the seven cases studied, there was a known history of threats of self-harm in four cases, while in the other three it could not be determined whether or not there had been prior threats.

One woman remembered her partner's previous response to her attempt to leave: 'When I left him [some years prior to the offence] he sat at the table and put a gun to his head. He said he would shoot himself. My brother talked him out of it.' In another case the woman described how difficult it had been to effect the separation because, even after the couple had agreed to end the relationship, she could not get her husband to leave: 'I had his belongings packed. He sat on the floor in the shed. He left letters—suicide letters. There were letters for each of us; for his parents, for me, and one for each of the children.'

Another survivor remembered being inundated with suicidal notes: 'He used to write suicide letters all the time. Every week I would get wills and other documents reading, "Open at a certain date". When I found out about my daughter being murdered, I burned everything. I didn't know I would need it later.' Another respondent indicated the separation had elicited threats of self-harm by her ex-partner, although he had not made any such threats previously. Finally, newspaper reports indicated that one perpetrator had made eight suicide threats by letter prior to abducting and killing his three children.

Threats of Harm to Others

In six cases there was a known history of various threats of harm should the wife succeed in leaving the relationship, but in the seventh it was not possible to determine whether or not such threats had been made. In some cases threats had been issued long before the final separation, and some had been present since the commencement of the relationship. One researcher comments:

> virtually all batterers make it clear both implicitly and explicitly that 'their' women are not free to leave the relationship. Not infrequently, batterers threaten to kill not only battered women but their children and their families if they try to leave (Ewing 1997: 23).

When Narelle was asked about prior threats made in relation to her safety, or the safety of others, she replied: 'He said before the separation, "If you ever leave, I'll kill you and the kids". He made it clear he wouldn't let another man have his kids.'

Ruth recalled that, although statements made to her in the past by her husband did not appear threatening at the time, on looking back she realised that they had been veiled threats: 'They weren't overt threats, but in hindsight they were threats. He used to say, "What would you do if I got the kids?" He confirmed that by "got" he meant kill them.'

Danni, discussing her perception that the perpetrator seemed to believe that his wife and his children were his possessions, also confirmed he made threats: 'Yes, he threatened to kill her several times. He said, "You're always mine. I'll own you forever."' Danni reported that Michael, the one surviving perpetrator in the study, had a history of threatening behaviour. She said: 'He had threatened his brother. He would also threaten with money. He tried to stop us putting a notice [in memoriam] in the paper two years ago. I put a big notice in the paper about the children.'

Sometimes the threats were veiled; at other times they were quite explicit. But even when they were explicit they were not always recognised or judged as such. This confirms the findings in the literature that victims of domestic violence tend to minimise violence and trauma as a way of coping with them (Deaton and Hertica 2001: 14–15).

Clare did not interpret her ex-partner's comment to his mother-in-law as a threat. He had said, 'Your day will come and you will find out what it is like to lose your little girl'. Perhaps her inability to recognise the threat was a result of her experience on other occasions when she had told people about her fears, because they had tended to minimise the risk to the children. She felt her lawyer had pressured her to agree to access even though Tom's behaviour was extremely irrational and his mental health was obviously deteriorating. On one occasion it seemed that he had come close to committing the offence: he rang his mother-in-law in a very distressed state saying that he and the children were in the bush. The grandmother could hear the children crying in the background, and when they were returned the older child had described how her father had tried to smother her. Clare reported: 'He had never threatened to harm them before this. My daughter told me he had put a pillow over her face and she had choked. He said she had choked on a biscuit.'

It is obvious in these cases that numerous threats were made and that the relatives, friends and associates of the perpetrator were aware of them, yet no-one took action in response to them. Ruth found out after the offence that Barry had made threats that she had been unaware of: 'He told his best mate two days before the offence that he was going to kill me. His [Barry's] family was in the room when he said it.' Nobody reported these threats to police or took any action to warn the woman of her husband's intention.

Circumstances Leading up to the Offence

It is clear the women had become used to placating their husbands and acquiescing to their demands, subordinating their own needs to those expressed by their husbands, even after leaving the relationship. Danni, an aunt of two of the children, reported:

> We had arranged for my mother's seventieth birthday party. We were having a big family party and wanted the children to be

there. She [the mother of the children] said that the children couldn't go because their father would chuck a tantrum. She said, 'He'll think we're playing games if we don't let them go on access'.

Danni made it clear that she believed the offence was premeditated:

> I think he planned it. He was invited to the party because we didn't want to exclude him. I thought it was weird that he wanted them [the children]. He was supposed to be going away on a fishing trip and there wasn't really time for a visit.

It appears these children were allowed to go with their father rather than attend the family gathering, because their mother was fearful of his reaction if she were to deny him contact. Understandably, this woman still suffers extreme guilt for allowing the children to go with their father.

Ruth said:

> For me personally it was out of the blue. I would never have believed he would do it. Although there were two occasions when I thought he might hurt the children. One was the night he took off with the children and didn't return them until 11.30 pm. The other was when, at 8.30 pm one night, two men were outside my house. They were pouring something out of a five-litre can onto my lawn, right next to my house. I rang the police. I said, I think my husband is trying to burn us to death. I had a migraine. The police found an oily residue on the road and on the lawn. They never investigated. I don't believe the police thought anything serious was going to happen. Later that night, at about 1.30 or 2 am, the offence was committed.

The mother of a three-year old girl who was killed said:

> He was seeing a woman who had lost a child. I wonder if in his warped brain he thought, 'That's how I can hurt her'? I'd got myself a car again, and he wanted to borrow it, but I refused. I knew he just wanted to smash it up like he had done to the car I had before.

Clare indicated major changes in Tom's behaviour prior to the offence:

> He lost weight. He got a tattoo which before he had always hated. He smoked. Before I left him he never smoked. He lit a joint. He never did this previously, and he started mixing with pub people, he had despised them before. He was drinking and on tablets as well. He went shopping and bought a hose. My child was killed by carbon monoxide being passed through a hose from the car into the vehicle.

As previously described, it appears that Tom had either rehearsed the killing or come very close to committing the offence on a previous contact visit with both children present, but had been dissuaded from this when he telephoned the children's grandmother who talked him into returning the children.

Narelle explained how her husband had collected the children prior to the offence.

> He came round the week after I left, early in the morning at six-thirty. He said: 'I'm going on a fishing trip with my mates and I want to have the children before I go away because I don't know how long I'll be gone'. He was different, like a robot. He was like a man on a mission. Our daughter didn't want to go. She screamed. I encouraged her to go. Then I never saw them again.

Danni recalled, 'He wasn't horrible, he was great, and he loved his kids. I think he was drinking the night before. He was with his sister the night before, who I believe was a very negative influence. He put alcohol in a Fanta bottle to make the children go to sleep before he killed them.'

Ruth explained how her husband had gained entry to her house after months of stalking her:

> It happened in the bedroom. He organised entry. When he returned he dismantled the inside of the toilet window. It was premeditated. It was premeditated since the day he was served

with the divorce papers. I signed them. He bought a gun the very next day and licensed it five days later. He forged a letter to get the gun. He bought the gun from a cop.

Clare raised the issue of the unsuitability of family members to supervise contact:

> I didn't know that on the first access he took the children to the beach unsupervised. The court order said his parents were supposed to supervise the access, due to my concerns, but they didn't do it. They didn't believe he was a threat to the children's safety.

Involvement with Services

As noted, it was not possible to determine with any certainty the full extent of community agency involvement with the families. For obvious reasons, there was more information about the wife's involvement with these agencies than the husband's.

The wife and children in one family were clients of Family and Children's Services and the children were patients of the Sexual Abuse Unit at Princess Margaret Hospital. Another child was being seen by a clinical psychologist at a children's clinic, having been diagnosed with attention deficit hyperactivity disorder. One couple had attended a church-based counselling service prior to separation.

I could not establish whether any of the perpetrators were being seen by a mental health specialist prior to the offence. One man had been prescribed anti-depressant medication, but whether this was prescribed by a psychiatrist or a general practitioner is not known.

Narelle, who had lived in the country, and who had tried in the past to seek counselling to address the long-standing problems within the marriage said: 'There was nothing [no counselling service] available in those days in the country. I didn't have counselling before the offence, your counsellor was your doctor.'

Research reveals that 'Perpetrators [of domestic violence] are unlikely to recognise that they have a problem unless some *major crisis* which disrupts or threatens their present situation occurs' (Elliot and

Shanahan 1988: 2). Some women reported trying to get their partners to attend counselling prior to separation but with no success. Clare wondered whether the men's support group that Tom had attended had had a negative effect on him, because she was aware that one of the other members had committed a serious violent offence against his ex-wife. 'He used to laugh at psychologists and psychiatrists.'

SUMMARY

All respondents indicated there had been difficulty in the woman leaving her partner and getting him to accept the termination of the relationship. In terms of the Family Court process, there were three cases where there had been no court involvement at all, although one of these couples had chosen to register a Deed of Agreement at the court registry. Only two couples had matters before the Family Court at the time of the offence that would have indicated a current active dispute in relation to custody or access.

There is some evidence from what happened after separation to suggest that, firstly, a lack of individuation on the part of the perpetrator may have been a precursor to the offences (although in at least two of the cases it was reported that the men had had extra-marital affairs). Some men spoke of being unable to contemplate a future without their partners and children, even though there had been a history of substantial conflict.

Secondly, violence had escalated after separation and in some cases took on new forms. It was commonly reported that perpetrators stalked their ex-partners and made threats to harm themselves and others. An observable deterioration in the perpetrators' mental health was commonly reported, but I could not confirm this with medical evidence.

Thirdly, it was not possible to determine the full extent of the families' involvement with community agencies such as the police, the courts and counselling services. This area is worthy of future study. Had agencies been involved, it could be useful to track what information each of them held about the situations in these families prior to the offence, to what extent they were sharing their knowledge, and whether they were jointly planning and coordinating their services to the families. This would be useful information to have for future planning to reduce risk.

CHAPTER — 5

The Aftermath

IMMEDIATE REACTIONS

It was very distressing for respondents to recall the events that immediately followed the deaths of the children, and it required a great deal of courage for them to do so. One woman, who expressed a range of powerful emotions and wept profusely throughout the interview, explained that she did not usually let go of her feelings to this extent, but that she had found this release of what she called pent-up emotion beneficial. She said: 'It's been good today [to be able to talk]. People think I'm strong, because I hide my feelings, but today is good 'cos I've had to sit and talk.'

One family member recalled that the family received news of the offence as they celebrated a birthday:

> We were at the party, having a great time. Halfway through the party, the police came. We were waving at them! They said they wanted to speak to the head of the family. My brother went. When he came back, we knew by the look on his face that it was the end of our lives.

The children's mother said she had been forcibly injected with sedatives before being told that her children had been murdered:

It was the day before New Year's Eve. All the family was at my grandmother's seventieth birthday. I stayed home waiting for the children [to return from contact]. Two doctors arrived, with detectives and police, and a priest. They jabbed me, stuck two needles in, one in each arm. They said my husband had had an accident. They wouldn't tell me at first, then they held me down and then said the children didn't survive.

A relative of this woman complained about her treatment, alleging the initial heavy sedation had been administered without consent. This relative held the strong view that subsequent heavy sedation of the mother with prescribed drugs to help her cope with the tragedy had, in fact, blocked her ability to fully experience the pain at the time, and had consequently impeded the healing process. The woman had then developed a long-term mental illness for which she still requires treatment. Her relative claimed there had been no previous sign of mental illness in the mother of the children. She said: 'They gave her too many drugs to deaden the pain. It sent her mental, now she's schizophrenic, and she wasn't before. They should have let her go through it and feel it, so she could heal.'

Clare sobbed as she reported that when her child died she heard a loud bang and felt a 'huge rocket' go through her chest. Simultaneously, she experienced a brilliant white light.

In two families the death of the children appears to have precipitated an additional family death; in one family it was the children's great-grandfather, in another the cousin of the perpetrator. Danni explained:

My father [the deceased children's great-grandfather] died the next day from a heart attack. The shock of the children [being murdered] killed him. The police asked me to identify him. I was calm, I said I couldn't do it. We had just lost two members of our family. It's too much when three people in your family die in two days.

In the other family, Michael had taken his children to the country, near where he and Narelle had lived before their separation, to kill them. Michael's extended family were farmers and lived close by, with properties close to one another. His cousin stumbled upon the vehicle in which Michael lay unconscious with his two murdered children. Narelle said: 'The man who found the kids was their father's first cousin. He [Michael] had taken them to where we used to go necking when we were young. That man had a heart attack less than two weeks later. It was so sad, he was a lovely man.'

LATER

In the first few weeks after the offences the families were in an acute state of shock. This may explain why, despite a search of the death and funeral notices in the newspaper archives, I could not find records for all those who died. Some families did not place notices in the papers for the children or the perpetrators.

Several women found out after the offence that others had known that the perpetrator had been stalking them, or had purchased items such as a gun, hoses, and restraints to assist in committing the offence. Those who had known were often described as friends or relatives of the perpetrator and had not shared this information. This led to a great deal of anger in survivors because they viewed these individuals as being culpable in some way or other for the offence.

After the offence one woman discovered things about her partner's previous actions which she had been unaware of. 'After it happened, I'd have girls come up to me and say, "I've had your husband at my house"—barmaids! He even made love to my best friend. Even now, I won't have a best friend.'

PATERNAL FAMILIES

In all cases where family members were interviewed, it was apparent that the offence had caused permanent alienation between the maternal and paternal families. In some cases members of the paternal family were excluded from the children's funeral. Some women reported having little or no contact with the paternal family after the offence. It is not known how the perpetrators' families coped with the aftermath of the offence because, as discussed, these families could not be located or contacted. It can be surmised from the evidence concerning the effects of the trauma on the members of the extended maternal family, their friends, and members of the community, that the paternal families' experiences of loss and trauma would be intense and far-reaching. In addition, the guilt typically experienced where someone has suicided would be compounded by the knowledge that family member had also murdered a defenceless child or children.

Narelle recalled: 'After a couple of days, you go to the police, you make a statement. His mum and dad were in the other room. They came and hugged me. I never saw them then, until the kids' funeral. Then I never saw them again.'

Clare had been relying on Tom's family to supervise her daughter's contact with him, a responsibility which they abandoned when they allowed him to drive off alone with the child. She said: 'I never see them. They didn't come to the funeral, I didn't want them there.'

LONG-TERM EFFECTS

I asked the respondents what long-term effects the offence had on them and their families. It was a difficult question to ask of people who had just related the details of a most traumatic and horrific crime, expressing sorrow, anger and a range of other intense emotions. On two occasions I decided the question was intrusive at that time, and asked it at a later date.

The answers ranged from the predictable to the most unexpected, and were often expressed with very raw emotion, even when the offence had happened many years before.

Survivors reported the offence did have long-term serious effects on them. One woman was unable to cope alone and had to live for years in the care of relatives, because she was unable to keep her medical and counselling appointments without substantial support. Insomnia was a common problem among survivors; again this endured for years after the offence, and in some cases survivors became reliant on alcohol or drugs to deal with it. Some of the drugs were prescribed by medical practitioners, but some survivors resorted to illegal drugs. Some of the women did go on to form new partnerships, and they saw the impact of the offence on the children they had later. Their extended families also experienced long-term effects. They reported examples of family members developing long-term mental illness and substance abuse problems.

As most of the women were young when their children were killed, there were significant issues for them in relation to fertility and future childbirth. Narelle explained that she was quite unable to undergo a tubal ligation, in spite of having had three subsequent children who were all alive and well.

> It has affected me. I can't get my tubes tied and yet I don't want any more children. It's self-preservation just in case. I tried to have it done, but I had to walk out of the clinic; years later, same thing again. Sitting in there, walked out! I couldn't do it just in case. I won't go back to the clinic again.

Clare saw herself as being a very different person to the woman she had been before the offence: 'Well I've probably changed. In my family they're very sensitive to deaths in the family. If you hear of something bad happening to a child it makes you cry.'

One survivor reported hearing that the perpetrator's father had become very ill after the offence, and she believed the shock and trauma of the event had caused this illness.

There were many reports of extreme anger in the extended families of the children who died. Danni said: 'My brother wants to kill him [the surviving perpetrator]. He doesn't believe he should have two more kids [from his subsequent marriage]. My other brother arranged the children's funeral and he feels the same.' She added that, in her family, there was a lack of trust when couples separated, even when there was no apparent threat to children. She said: 'Women in the family are very sensitive. They won't give their kids over to anyone. One niece won't let her kids go on access visits.'

The Mothers

Predictably, the mothers of the murdered children appeared to have suffered the most. Involvement in later relationships, and even the birth of subsequent children, did not appear to lessen their pain. One respondent told how the family had fought to prevent the children's mother from killing herself. They took it in turns to care for her, as she had no interest in surviving without her children. One said, of the children's mother, 'She has tried to suicide so many times, I've lost count'.

One woman reported that five years after the offence she felt immobilised, at times, by a combination of grief and anger, and was unable sometimes to mix with others or to leave her house: 'I've got good days and bad days. Some days I don't want to go downtown.' Another recalled:

After it happened I didn't go out of the house for three years. I never went inside a shop for three years. I was on Mogadon and Valium. I looked at myself one day and I was grey. It was all the drugs I was on. My mum got me and made me look in the mirror. She said, 'You can either kill yourself, or get on with life'. I decided to get on with life. I got off the drugs, I did it myself. I got a job in a shop a few years after it happened.

Clare said:

I tend to cry at night when there's no-one here. When my husband is on night shift. The sad thing is, sometimes I want to cry and I can't. I look at the photos and it hurts so much, but I can't cry. Then I feel guilty. I think I should be able to. Time evolves. You learn to continue daily duties. I still have numb days. The wound is still there. The knife is still in it. I'm on an emotional roller coaster.

Women reported physical ailments, in addition to depression and other mental illness, as a direct result of the offence. These are some of their comments:

The worst thing is the misconception of stress. I've had anxiety attacks.

I have very high blood pressure.

My periods go out of kilter.

I get pain in my chest.

My hair falls out. I was frightened to wash my hair too vigorously, 'cos it would fall out.

I lost a lot of weight.

Some days I go to the cemetery. I feel like a block of concrete. I feel like I can't even walk there. I feel so angry.

I keep myself busy, by working. It helps.

Sometimes you feel guilty 'cos you go a couple of days without thinking of them but...

One woman wept as she explained how her grief had prevented her from keeping pace with the growth and development of her subsequent children. She said: 'My memories! I've gone through life so fast. I don't know where I've been. I've only just bought a camera to take photos of my youngest child [now three years old].' Another said:

My husband has learned to read me well. If I go three days [bottling up emotions] then the anger eats you alive. You can try to stay soft but I can truly feel the anger flowing in my veins. You want to get it out, but you can't. Your head feels ready to explode. The next day you feel weak.

One woman described a frightening, apparently paranormal, experience where she felt that the perpetrator had visited her after his death. She wondered if this had been a ghost presence. She described feeling as if he had been forced to experience the effects of his actions, through her:

> Once, I felt something cold behind me. It was him. He was look-ing in my eyes, in my hair. I couldn't move. I felt locked. It was like I was feeling his emotion. I couldn't believe what I [as him] had done. The pain was so deep. I [as him] looked over at the photos of our daughter. I was so frightened! How quickly your mind can get absorbed, you can quickly go from being normal to being in a breakdown. I was so scared! What scared me was I couldn't move, so he had to feel what I felt.

All respondents reported feeling some level of guilt for not seeing the risk to the children, or for failing to protect them. They also expressed extreme anger towards others who, they thought, should have protected the children. Clare said:

> I'll never forgive myself. I told him to bring her back. He said he'd never hurt them! She told me he had put a pillow over her face. He said she choked on a biscuit! Why would I ask someone to super-vise? She was three, she knew the difference between a pillow and a biscuit. Know what I hate? No-one had to swear on oath. No-one had to be responsible. They [his family] were not made to go to court for failing to provide supervision. If someone on super-vised contact goes out of sight they should be followed. Those bastards in his family knew he was gone for seven hours. They didn't even look. My overwhelming feeling is anger. It's eating me away. I know he planned it. I feel frustrated. He made the mess, now I've got to clean it up.

It was clear the offences caused long-term changes in the way that family members functioned. One woman described how, five years after the offence, she still felt she had a long way to go in order to resolve her anger and grief: 'I'm all emotional and I feel I'm not halfway through it'.

Another woman reported: 'About every eighteen months I go through something [major breakdown]. I need therapy.'

Danni said: 'She [the mother of victims] can't keep appointments with her psychiatrist. She is a victim. She can't do anything. We do everything, me and her sister. We share, we do all her paperwork, get her to her appointments.'

One respondent explained that her relative suffered a severe mental breakdown after the offence, which recurs at significant times of the year such as the children's birthdays, or at Christmas: 'She has nightmares of Fanta bottles coming at her. It's always the same nightmare.' The perpetrator had sedated the children with alcohol mixed in Fanta. The relative continued:

> She goes off [experiences severe mental illness] at Christmas and on birthdays. Once they had the tactical response group chasing her through the bush. In the asylum she met a guy and had it off. She got pregnant [and had a daughter] but her sister looks after the child because if the child gets sick her mother cannot cope.

The woman herself confirmed that the sight of this popular soft drink still distressed her: 'I can't stand seeing Fanta bottles'. She finds that the smell of exhaust fumes still causes her to react strongly, even though the offence happened many years ago. 'I pull up at the lights and smell the fumes of the car in front. I get distressed. I think to myself, I hope no-one can see.'

One respondent said of her relative, 'She can't listen to a certain band because little Martin [who was murdered] used to hum a tune, it went, "Throw down your guns—don't you be so reckless". It feels like it was an omen.'

The Children

The reports of the effects on children in the families studied were especially poignant. One mother said, 'The kids at school ask them [half-siblings of the murdered children] questions like "How were the children killed?"'

The mother of the one surviving child described the problems he had experienced in adjusting to his sister's death. She described how one day she and her son were walking down the street:

> Her brother saw a little girl that looked like his sister. He ran over and called to her. She was with her father. When my son found it was not his sister he became very upset, I was crying. The child's father must have thought we were mad.

This child was described as having long-term behavioural and emotional problems as a direct result of his sister's murder.

> He has nightmares. I can't get him out of it. He was a bedwetter, now he gets up and wees on the floor. He is a bully. He probably got his anger from me. There is something wrong with him. We can have no Christmas with her. How can her brother accept it? How selfish of their father not to think of that for our son!

Children in the extended family were also affected. Where there was marital separation in the extended family, some were never allowed to go on unsupervised contact to their fathers, because of family fears about the possibility of harm occurring to them, even though there was nothing to indicate any risk to them from their father.

One woman explained the children in her family believed her murdered daughter was now up in the heavens and would look at the sky and wave to a star which they believed to be their sister.

The Extended Family

Each person interviewed reported reliving the trauma of the offence each time they became aware of another familicide being committed, and they described themselves as being over-protective of children. One commented: 'When there is another one [familicide] my brother says "Another selfish prick"'. And as we have seen, one relative commented that the women of the maternal family were very sensitive and wouldn't hand their children over to anyone.

One woman reported that some members of her family had increased their alcohol consumption since the offence. She also described how the mother of the children had suffered badly from insomnia for years. Someone had suggested to her that marijuana might help, but no-one in the family knew anything about the drug or how to obtain it. The woman sought out the necessary information herself and then found someone to purchase it from, even though she regarded the task as very risky because it put her in touch with people who were professional dealers. She was concerned about getting found out by the police and being charged with an offence:

> Marijuana helps her get to sleep. I go out and get it for her, she wouldn't know how to get it. I didn't either, but I found out. You meet people you wouldn't normally meet or see. Not people you want to mix with. I get it for her, but I'm scared of getting caught …My dad died, the kids died, I was left nursing my dying mother. I was only twenty-four. So marijuana helped me too when I needed it. The doctor said he would prescribe it if he could.

Some family members appeared to have coped by using various forms of denial. An aunt of two of the children was reported to keep herself exceptionally busy, while their grandmother had found religion, become a missionary and gone to work with disadvantaged children overseas. The children's mother, who was very open to talking about the effects of the offence on her family, said: 'My mum and sister don't want to talk about it. My sister hides a lot. She keeps going, keeps busy, doesn't deal with it.'

EXPLAINING THE OFFENCE

Respondents were asked, 'How do members of your family explain the offence?' These are some of their responses:

> They don't, they shake their heads. The men can't see how, can't get over how, he could do it. They can't get over it. They don't use

the word 'murder', they say, 'When [the children] passed'. They say, '*The Day*'. They say, '*That Day*'. Everyone in the family knows what '*That Day*' means. She and the kids belonged to him. That's why he murdered them, to make her suffer, to punish her for leaving. If he'd thought it would hurt her more to kill her, he would have. But it hurts more for her to live with the children gone. That is why he did it, to hurt her. I've never made sense of it. This is what sent me off studying psychology, to try to understand it.

All respondents reported feeling changed significantly by their experience. They found it hard when others expected them to 'get over it'. One survivor had met a woman whose son was killed in an accident. 'People were saying she should get over it. I get angry when people say that. How can you get over it? It's like having a life that should be pushed under the mat.' Others said:

> People want me to be the same as before but I feel like saying to them, 'I have had two kids who have been murdered. I need you to understand that and get on. I can't be the same.'

> I still get upset. I'm supposed to be a different person. It was many years ago now, but they want me to be who I was before it happened. Some people acknowledge it, some people don't. Maybe the trauma is too much. They're suffering more because they can't express it.

> It killed us, it killed our family, but it's not just us who were affected. It's like a pebble in a pond. The ripples are still pulsating. It destroyed our whole family!

In spite of all this there were some positive comments about the effect of the trauma.

> A gift is given back, wisdom, strength, compassion.

> You appreciate everything a bit better. You treat your children better.

You treat all children better. Even food tastes better.

You value children more, you can't say 'No' to children.

Narelle said: 'My brother-in-law sits me down. He says, "I try to comprehend what you've been through. You're the strongest person I know—to get up every morning and smile at the kids [her nephews and nieces]."' She smiled and added, 'That makes me feel better!'

Survivors' Feelings Towards the Perpetrator and Paternal Families

Members of one family reported feeling harassed by the one surviving perpetrator, Michael, who would regularly ring and ask the family for forgiveness. One said: 'He rings my nephew. He wants us to forgive him but we never will. He asked for her to forgive him. She won't!' The children's mother said: 'He writes letters wanting my forgiveness in writing. I won't give it.'

Others reported:

We will never forgive him.

I hate him so much, I can't get the anger out! For five years I've been so angry!

My brother used to visit him in prison. They had a big blue. My brother found out how selfish he was. Then he [brother] apologised to me for visiting.

They [my family] hate him. Mum used to feel sorry for him. How can a man go from being a father to doing that? He was over-protective and overbearing. My mum thinks he was callous and gutless.

My brothers want to kill him.

It is understandable that the offences caused an enduring rift between the children's maternal and paternal families. None of the maternal families interviewed had contact with members of the paternal family, except in the case where the perpetrator survived. This contact, initiated by the perpetrator, appears to always occur following publicity of an incident of familicide, and consists of the perpetrator seeking forgiveness from his ex-partner and her family. The maternal family in this case were resolute that he would never be forgiven.

When asked how the paternal family had coped, other respondents replied:

> I wouldn't know. I never see them. They didn't come to her funeral. I didn't want them there.

> I've never heard from them. They try to cover it up. It's an emotional issue. They come from a small town. They own half the town. If you went today, if you mentioned it, you'd be shunned. They are on his side. When I tried to put a memorial in the paper, they tried to stop me. I said, 'Is it upsetting Mr —— [the paternal grandfather]?' They had to print it!

> I have never spoken to his family since the offence.

> I have spasms of wanting to kill him [the surviving perpetrator] when I have my periods.

> When I see her [the surviving mother of the children] down and out, that's when I want to kill him.

SUMMARY

It is clear that the effects of familicide on the extended family of the victims are severe and of long duration. They range from chronic mood disturbance, depression and other mental illness to increased use of alcohol and drugs. Post-traumatic stress symptoms such as nightmares, intrusive thoughts, avoidance of trigger stimuli and over-protection of children were commonly reported. All respondents saw their families as having experienced irreversible change as a result of the offence. Several survivors believed they would never fully recover from the event, and one, suffering acute guilt over her children's deaths, did not believe she deserved to recover. It is likely that the families of the perpetrators suffer in similar ways.

CHAPTER 6

The Context

This chapter examines the offences with the benefit of hindsight, reviewing the role of community agencies, counsellors, police, courts and family members, and asks what could have been done differently. It concludes with the survivors' views of their futures.

Community Agency Involvement

Some families had involvement with various community agencies before the offence, and one couple had used marriage counselling. Other couples had no agency involvement at all. In some cases I could not find out whether couples had sought agency assistance.

Several women had on-going contact with the police in relation to their partner's stalking or violent behaviour. They described this contact as very unsatisfactory, and unfortunately police involvement was ineffective in preventing the deaths of the children. In Peter's case it appears that the lack of co-ordination of police services helped to enable him to evade the police chase and kill his three children before committing suicide.

In general, there was little involvement with counselling agencies, except the compulsory attendance at the Family Court Counselling Service for those who had applied to the court. It is possible greater access to counselling might have alleviated the emotional distress that was a common experience of both partners following separation. Some respondents raised questions about the type of support offered by men's groups, expressing the perception that some groups fuelled anger and bitterness in men who had not come to terms with their wives' departure.

Survivors' Explanations of Why it Happened

Because I could not interview any surviving perpetrators about their motive for familicide, I asked respondents for their views about the cause of the offence.

All respondents referred to the perpetrator as having an obsession about his female partner, but they varied in their attempts to identify the motivation for the offences or offer an explanation for them. When asked, Clare said: 'It's motivated by obsession, and possession'.

Ruth agreed with Clare, but also felt strongly that the compulsion on the non-custodial parent to pay child support was a related factor. Under current Australian arrangements for child support, the custodial parent applies for financial assistance from the social security agency, Centrelink. The applicant is required to provide the name and employment details of the child's other parent, and the Child Support Agency may then deduct child support from that person's wages and pay it to the custodial parent.

Ruth believed that, at one level, child support gives the custodial parent autonomy and enhances separation of the family unit. However, she felt that, at another level, child support feeds the notion of ownership. She believed that a woman who applies for child support is forced into a process that may work against her own self-interest. Ruth said she felt men resented having to pay child support and often blamed their wives for claiming it. Women are put in an unenviable position: if they do not apply for child support, they surrender their right to Supporting Parents Benefit. Ruth felt strongly that men do not acknowledge that it is the government which acts to get the money, not the ex-wife. She summarised: 'It's about possession, obsession and child support. This is a huge issue as these three factors interact.'

One woman told me that some recent UK studies show parental homicide increases where child support is compulsory. I could not locate the studies so I could not verify this. Other women believed that applying for child support definitely increased the risk for them and for their children. In fact, one woman was so concerned about her ex-husband's response to a claim for child support that she lied to the authorities, telling them that he was paying child support to her when in fact he was not. She said: 'I put on the Centrelink form that he paid me, but he didn't. I didn't want any reason for him to come back at me for anything. It's not worth squabbling.'

Further evidence for the existence of this proprietary attitude of men towards their families comes from research undertaken in 1986. It found that men often feel resentment and anger because their wives are able to access benefits to enable them to live independently. One man was reported as stating: 'It's the government's fault. If they didn't give them pensions, they couldn't leave and there wouldn't be a problem' (Elliott and Shanahan 1988: 10).

Narelle saw it differently. She said: 'I think it was Michael's selfishness. He did the most selfish act he could do. He was just thinking how could he cope [with losing his wife and kids]? I don't think it was revenge.' However, Narelle's family strongly disagreed with her explanation. They held the view that the murder of the children had been Michael's revenge on her for leaving him. Family members were mindful of his threats, in the years preceding separation, to kill both his wife and the children if she dared to leave him.

Some women blamed themselves, feeling that some inadequacy of theirs might have precipitated the offence. Narelle appeared to have tried over and over to keep her marriage together, and had witnessed her husband's violent behaviour and infidelity over many years before finally leaving. She broke down and cried in great distress: 'I've got all the guilt. I'm the cause of it all. If only I'd made a better marriage. If only I'd worked harder, the person who found the kids wouldn't have had a heart attack, wouldn't have died.' When I asked what she meant by this, Narelle tearfully explained: 'I think that's what his family think. I think everybody thinks that…It's what I think.'

Clare explained Tom's offence in this way:

I think, you're a family for twenty-four hours a day. Then, losing it, they [men] can't deal with it. Tom was too busy arguing. He didn't think of the effect on the children. It was a stupid tug-of-war. They were possessions taken away from him. He didn't think of the welfare of the children. I bent over backwards for him to see the children. Looking back now, I was too stressed. I couldn't see the whole picture. I know now he was planning it for a long time. I wish I hadn't let him have her for Christmas. I thought I had a life-time of Christmases.

It was clear from reading the Family Court files and the newspaper reports, as well as from listening to respondents, that in the majority of cases the men exhibited a proprietary attitude towards their partners and their children. Danni recalled: 'He told her, "You're always mine. I'll own you forever."' The ex-partner of Michael, the surviving perpetrator, said:

It's in their heads. When they go through something, lose a wife, kids, something inside tips [the balance], but to the point where you'd put the exhaust into the car? You'd have to be very low. He's suffering every day. I know that 'cos I wake up with it every day.

Clare said of her family: 'They don't understand how you can go from being a father to doing that [committing familicide]. He was over-protective and overbearing. My mother thinks he was callous and gutless.'

Danni, an aunt of two of the murdered children, said:

They were possessions, she and the kids belonged to him. We think it was revenge. I've never made sense of it. That's what sent me off studying psychology to try to understand. Now [after studying] I see that crack [defect] in other men. He murdered them to make her suffer. This is why he did it. To hurt her. If he'd thought it would hurt her more to kill her, he would have. But it hurts her more to live with the children gone. My sister and brother think like me, they agree, it was premeditated.

She added: 'He could never talk about his feelings. They belonged to him, she and the kids belonged to him. That's why he murdered them.'

One family member thought that Michael had killed his two children from fear that their mother would not care for them properly after separation, even though Narelle had always been the primary caregiver whereas he had often abrogated his parental and spousal responsibilities. 'He murdered on an assumption. He thought she wasn't going to be a good mother' she claimed.

Another woman was very clear that her husband had murdered the children to pay her back for leaving him. She said: 'It was revenge'.

WHAT COULD HAVE PREVENTED THE OFFENCE?

The Women's Coalition Against Family Violence, discussing case studies of spousal and child homicide committed by men, reported on the inaction by community agencies:

> These accounts highlight the extent of institutional and community inaction towards, and therefore complicity in, domestic violence. They also make it clear that the killings were not merely inexplicable or aberrant occurrences, and they did not occur as a result of drunkenness, stress, conflict, madness, 'provocation' or any of the many other ostensible reasons we so frequently hear from the courts and the media. Rather, the killings were the end point of strategies used by men to control and dominate their wives, girlfriends, ex-partners and children (1994: vii).

The Role of Counselling Agencies

Now we will look at survivors' perceptions of the role of various community agencies in failing to prevent the offence. It was clear there was some naivety about available services and their role. It is likely the perceptions were influenced, in each case, by how much time had elapsed since the offence, and what stage each respondent had reached in terms of resolving the suffering.

Asked what could have been done by their families, or by community agencies, to prevent the offence, respondents' accounts varied. In relation to support services for men having difficulty coping with separation, Ruth stated:

> All support should be based on the ethos that violence is not condoned. Support should uphold that women and children are not possessions. Support should be provided by not discounting women who make allegations against men [especially in the Family Court] as being mean, money-grubbing, or vindictive bitches.

Some women made clear their belief that nothing could have been done to prevent the offence. Narelle thought access to counselling might have helped, but she and her family lived in the country and there was no such service there at the time. She said: 'If there would have been more public marriage counselling maybe we could've gone, but there was none'.

The Role of the Police

Narelle's previous attempts to leave Michael had been met with violence. Asked if the police might have been able to prevent the offence, she said Michael had not reacted violently on the final occasion and had given the appearance of accepting her departure. She said: 'I had no reason to go to the police'.

Ruth, who had reported her husband's stalking behaviour numerous times, said:

> There is a need to document telephone calls. I had made dozens of telephone calls to the police. I gave up in the end. I asked to be included in their drive-by list. I gave them his vehicle's registration number. They never put my name in the drive-by book. No-one came forward and said he had a history of stalking. Basically, when a woman says she is terrified, they should treat it as a potential homicide. There were no investigations of my complaints on some occasions. At the time of the offence, there was no time to investi-

gate. He drew out a large amount of money that afternoon [preceding the offence]. It is highly possible he paid someone [to assist in the offence]. The money was never found.

Clare had made numerous complaints to the police about her ex-husband, Tom, stalking and harassing her. As we have seen, she felt traumatised when the police removed him from the ceiling space of her house, where he had been concealed for some time. Her distress was increased by the way the police dealt with Tom after getting him down. Later, after Tom abducted their daughter, she believes the police were hesitant to begin searching. Her feelings are manifest:

They drove him out of town. They put him on a train. They put him on a bus. They let him shower in my bathroom because he was filthy. I felt violated! Why didn't the police have a logbook? Why didn't it come to court? Why didn't they charge him? They didn't go looking [when the children, on an earlier occasion, were not returned from access] because I wasn't hysterical. I couldn't believe it. The police could have been different. He was trying to break into my house. He had broken the Restraining Order so many times.

The Role of the Courts

Ruth said of the Court of Petty Sessions: 'I had a Restraining Order. At the point of appeal I dropped it, because his lawyer intimidated me, because no-one would testify against Barry.' Ruth said she would like to tell magistrates that they should have more training to help them to recognise the manipulative nature of the perpetrator. 'The magistrate said of Barry, "His lawyer has assured me he will stop harassing. I will drop or lapse the Restraining Order." Ten days later Barry was outside my house again.' Ruth believes that Barry had intended to burn her house down while she and the children slept, but when heavy rain on the night foiled his plan, he resorted to shooting them.

Women commented on the apparent inability of the court to fully understand emotional disturbance resulting from separation, and the associated risks this posed to families, as well as the court's impotence in restricting the behaviour of disturbed individuals. One said: 'The Family Court could do nothing!' Restraining Orders were seen as virtually useless. Breaches of Family Court orders rarely incurred penalties. When referring to her experience of the Family Court, Clare said: 'There are so many loopholes. The court doesn't protect people. The judges are so lenient.' Criticisms of the Family Court included lawyers and the mandatory counselling service. Women reported being pressured by their lawyers to agree, in counselling, to access arrangements which they did not believe provided safety for their children. They were told to agree, they said, because the court might perceive a refusal as unreasonable, leading ultimately to a worse outcome for them.

They also complained that the lack of power they felt, both in the marital relationship and in their relationship with the court, did not allow them to be open or honest about their concerns for their own or their children's safety. Referring to her experiences at the Family Court Counselling Service, Clare said: 'Why did I have to go to counselling? Why did I have to sit in the same room with him?' She challenged the confidentiality of counselling in the Family Court setting, saying: 'The counsellor could surely have let the magistrate know that Tom needed counselling and had problems'. Unfortunately, this is not so. Family Court counselling is confidential, and counsellors are not permitted to provide this type of information to the judiciary. Information on the court file already indicated that Tom was not coping with separation.

When asked whether a psychiatric report might have helped the Family Court to determine her case, given Tom's extremely disturbed behaviour before the offence, Clare replied: 'I don't know, because I don't know what's in a psychiatric report. I can't comment. But then some people are on the borderline. They only act psychotic when they are emotional.'

The Role of Family Members

Ruth reflected on the concerns she had articulated to friends and family about changes in her ex-husband's demeanour and stalking behaviour:

No-one believed me, not his family or mine. Take this [as they like to call it] 'out of character' behaviour; it shouldn't be accepted as normal behaviour. They were his ways of asking for help. But he didn't know how to ask for it, or accept it. Treatment should have been mandatory.

Narelle spoke about her ex-husband's reluctance to seek professional help with his feelings about the separation. She said: 'The night before he killed the children he was with a negative person. Maybe if he had been with a positive person, someone who could have told him how life goes on, then maybe…?'

WHAT HELPED THE SURVIVORS

Survivors described a range of ways they were helped after the offence. Those who had received counselling generally saw it as helpful, although there were some exceptions. They suggested how these services could be made more effective (see the recommendations in Chapter 8). Some women received counselling from several different sources, and maintained links with counselling services for years after the offence. Clare said: 'I had counselling from my doctor. He's a nice man, he really cares. The Victim Support Service saw me three or four times. My husband's employer sent a counsellor. I see a psychologist, he's a straight talker, he's helpful.'

Survivors reported it was not helpful when counsellors told them they knew or could understand how they felt. Such statements reduced the credibility of the counsellor, diminished rapport, and damaged the therapeutic relationship. Ruth acknowledged the offence was traumatic for the professional staff as well as for family members, but saw there was a lack of knowledge or understanding about how best to help: 'They tried to tell me how I felt. How could they know? Not many people have had this experience, thank God. No-one knew what to do. The clinical psychologists were hopeless. A female chaplain came in, she was wonderful.' Ruth said the chaplain, who acknowledged she had no idea what Ruth was experiencing or how to help her, was in retrospect the most helpful.

One family reported there was very little help available after the offence, because it happened before the Victim Support Service had been set up. The mother of the children in this family said: 'My family and this young priest came every day. I didn't really want them to come, but I knew they would, so I made a bit of an effort 'cos you just really want to die.' Her family and the priest appeared to be her only avenues of support.

Narelle, who is still in receipt of health services, said that, in terms of healing, for her, 'The best thing was to look at the sea'. She explained she had sought to be near the ocean every day for months after the offence, where she found the rhythm of the waves helped to soothe and heal her.

> The best thing was to look at the sea. I still go to the sea and look at the water and see the waves go in and out. I used to sit and watch it all day. I wouldn't notice that someone had been there. I'd look down and there would be a dinner or a drink. My family would bring it. I'd stay there all day, every day. I met a fisherman. I told him it all. I blurted it all out. He came every day. He'd check on me, check I was okay. That helped me. I run into him sometimes, with his wife. He says to his wife, 'This is the special lady I told you about'.

It appeared that the women were obliged to find their own ways to heal, because their suffering was so deep and intense that existing services lacked the experience or capacity to deliver what was needed. The survivors' families came and went in a haze, and were no doubt affected by their own grief and by the lack of services. Overall, I was left with the feeling that the survivors' families were all, in some ways, isolated by their own trauma, and the inability of others to meet their needs.

Criticisms of Services

Respondents were critical of the delivery of services. They perceived a lack of understanding by counselling agencies of the effects of the trauma on families. For example, the Victim Support Service contacted the survivors at a time when they were too shocked to understand what the service was or what it could offer, leading some to refuse its help without comprehending what was being offered. Some said they had no recollection of the service contacting them, even though they were assured contact had been made: 'I found out the VSS existed. They said they had contacted. They didn't contact. Everything was in a haze, I didn't remember.'

Respondents also felt there was not enough follow-up by the Victim Support Service. After two contacts it would withdraw if the woman refused help or was not able to respond to the approach. The interviewees said repeatedly they needed the service three, six, or even more, months down the track, when friends and extended family were needing to pull back their support in order to get on with their own lives. By this time survivors were often ready to make use of services, but had forgotten, or not registered, what had been offered. In looking back, survivors commented that they wished their refusals of help had been ignored, and that services had continued to be offered. They could see these had been needed and would have been helpful.

They also commented about the need for practical assistance. For example, Ruth experienced many difficulties as a result of her injuries, in addition to the emotional ones shared by all survivors: 'I had to peg out my washing and do housework with one leg. There was no help. No Silver Chain, no Meals on Wheels. Silver Chain said, "By the time your name comes up on the waiting list, you will have your prosthesis anyway".'

The nine-to-five weekday availability of services was also criticised. Night time, especially the early hours of the morning, was said to be a highly stressful time for survivors, and insomnia was a common problem.

What Services Should be Available?

Respondents said that, immediately after the offence, their anguish was so great that normal attempts at engagement by helping professionals were neither useful nor appropriate. Some said they had felt the need for someone just to be there, not to provide counselling or to intervene, and that the process of building rapport with such a person in these circumstances might take months. They thought this process would need to take place before any counselling began. One woman said: 'It's not about doing. It's about being.'

Danni felt strongly: 'There should be a support team, whether the family want it or not. I mean, to check on them in their own home. We were crumbling apart and there was no help.' Narelle agreed: 'There should be heaps of help. A network of people to keep communicating.' Respondents acknowledged that they had been difficult to help, because of their intense suffering and their ignorance about the services that were being offered. Narelle, who experienced extreme emotional withdrawal after the offence and had difficulty communicating at the time, even with her family, reiterated: 'Even if you say No [you don't want help] they should come anyway. You should have someone come every day, just to put a vase of flowers on the table to make you look at life.'

Ruth spoke of the need for practical support: 'I had to unpack my house from a wheelchair. Who do you ask for help? My friends couldn't cope. They'd see one thing [toy or other belonging] from the kids and burst into tears.' She had heard that, after similar offences in the United Kingdom, a worker would come each day to make sure that the survivor had basic food supplies such as bread and milk, and remembered to pay bills for essential services such as water and electricity. She believed this would have been a valuable service for her. As she reflected, individuals who are trying to recover from trauma often forget mundane tasks such as paying bills, but if services are then cut off it becomes a major task to have them reinstated. She explained: 'You are inundated with literature. A lot of legal stuff needs attention. You need someone to actively ensure that you understand the legal implications of documents you may sign. You need someone to go shopping.'

Clare had responded to the lack of appropriate services to assist her with her loss by putting a great deal of time and energy into helping other bereaved mothers. She said:

> I set up a support group for mothers. It was also open to siblings and grandparents. One-to-one counselling is good but support

groups are good too, because you don't have to talk. You can just listen. I like having my own confidante. Counselling is [only available] nine to five. Counselling is needed in the middle of the night. Professionals waited for us to get help for ourselves, but we didn't know what we needed.

Another area of concern is the lack of support for paternal families and for any surviving perpetrators. For the Victim Support Service to assist them could be misconstrued as a conflict of interest, and it would be inappropriate given the distress experienced by the maternal families. However, it is an area of need. Research is required to examine the experience of paternal families after the offence, establish their needs, and find out whether existing services can meet them. It is possible that guilt and shame may deter paternal family members from seeking assistance. As with maternal families, researchers and agencies need to show great sensitivity.

Other Reflections by Survivors

Women openly admitted their ability to form and sustain relationships with men were irreparably damaged. Guilt was a common theme among survivors. One said, 'I still have the guilts about the children. My daughter would be twenty-one this year. My son would be twenty. I don't think I deserve to get fixed [by counselling].'

Another reported:

Maybe I had a few problems before the children were killed. My problem was low self-esteem, not having a dad. My dad died when I was born. We were thrown out of the house every weekend by our stepfather when I was only sixteen. Maybe it comes from Mum, not loving myself. Mum had a whirling twirling door of men, young men. I'm a bit funny with men. That's why I'm not myself. My sister thinks I'm a crazy woman.

Two women reported being unable to undergo tubal ligation, even though they had no intention of having more children.

Clare wondered whether Tom's possessiveness towards her was a result of his first wife's infidelity, but conversely, she did not identify his behaviour towards her as a repeat of his treatment of his first wife. 'His first wife had an affair; maybe that's why he was so possessive. He used to follow her around. I don't know if she knew, but he used to follow her around and punch light poles out of anger.' Tom also followed Clare around after their separation, and hung about for hours outside her house, before finally hiding in her ceiling until removed by police. Clare reflected on the effect which the offence had on her:

> My life went in just one night. It took them a year to come up with the cause of death for my daughter, because they had to run so many tests. I wasn't allowed to kiss her goodbye. I couldn't give her a last kiss. They didn't want me to see her like that. I guess that's why I can't deal with anything. She's never going to come back.

Two women mentioned that, although they had managed to find new partners and had borne more children, their ability to parent had been compromised by their experience. One said: 'When I was going through a bad time with my new partner, I asked the girls' father to have them until I got myself together. They went to live with him two years ago.' This woman sobbed as she explained she was not able to look after the two children from this subsequent relationship, because of the mental illness she had suffered since the offence. She reluctantly acknowledged it was unlikely these children would ever return into her full-time care, as they are being well cared for and nurtured by their father and his new partner. A relative said: 'She married again, he's a lovely guy. They had two children, but in the end he had to take them away. He couldn't cope with her illness and her "going off" on birthdays etc.'

One woman felt that the term used by the Family Court to describe her child from her de facto relationship was demeaning: 'I didn't like them referring to her as an ex-nuptial child. It felt like a stigma.'

Narelle thinks often about the possibility of a chance meeting with her ex-husband Michael, who survived the offence. She is worried he may force her into a confrontation. As we have seen, he regularly contacts her family. She fears that he will contact her in person, not by chance but by design: 'I don't want him near here. I don't want to run into him in K-Mart. I might faint if I saw him. It might be too much. He will be in contact. I can feel it. He will make me have a confrontation.'

It is worth restating the major points. The families had little involvement with community agencies before the offence. Overall, neither the police nor the courts were effective in ensuring the safety of the women, even when there was a known history of threats to harm or kill. As many other studies have reported, Restraining Orders were hard to obtain and were ineffective when they were made (Websdale 1999: 51; Johnson 2002: 131; Martin 1978: 118).

Respondents felt let down by lawyers, the Family Court and the Family Court Counselling Service. They reported that even their own lawyers did not take threats of violence seriously. They felt it inappropriate to require women to attend court counselling jointly with their partners when there had been threats or actual violence. The respondents were disappointed in the court and the legal system, feeling that they were put under pressure or treated off-handedly. This highlights the court's inconsistencies and lack of knowledge in the area of domestic violence.

There is great scope for improvements in the manner of delivering victim services, in the education provided to legal officers and the judiciary, and in the police response to cases of stalking and domestic violence.

LOOKING FORWARD

All respondents were able to contemplate a future, but in every case they saw that future as significantly changed by the offence. Typical comments were:

I'm so scared. That's why I don't have a boyfriend.

I don't think I'll be with anyone forever 'cos of my problems.

But it makes you a better person.

I can't say no to children. I'm sure I could breastfeed a baby, if it needed it I could bring on milk.

You see into the future at a young age when you're going through a bad time.

When my kids were murdered, my gran said, 'You didn't get yourself fixed up did you?' I thought, 'How can you ask that so soon?' Now I understand. She said, 'These children [from a subsequent relationship] will save your life. Your babies will stop you sinking.'

I'm scared I'll stuff it up with L— [the child from subsequent relationship]. I don't want her to grow up under-confident like me. I don't want her to see what I go through every eighteen months.

It won't end for me until he [surviving child] dies. The sad thing for him [child] is that it won't end for him until he dies.

I told his wife—he met her in jail—that she will never be able to leave him. They have children. The children's mother has no children.

It has to change…

SUMMARY

Clearly, when the respondents looked back, they could see there had been warning signs which were either not recognised or ignored. The result was trans-generational trauma spread through the extended family, friends and others with devastating effect. Respondents reported that the future for themselves and their families was changed significantly, and irrevocably, by the offence.

Comparisons

Due to the dearth of research dealing specifically with familicide, the only way to approach this offence is to study the related areas of homicide (particularly spousal and filial homicide), and suicide as it relates to family killings. As familicide consists of both homicidal and suicidal acts, this research is highly relevant. Many of the features of spousal homicide are known to be similar to those of familicide: for example, the propensity of perpetrators to suicide after committing the offence, and the link between separation of intimates and the homicide event. When I began this study, I did not know how filicide in general related to child killing in familicide. Therefore, I also studied the literature on filicide in an attempt to understand the similarities and differences of these two categories.

HOMICIDE

Homicide is the ultimate crime of violence. Six of the seven cases in this study had a known history of violence, and in five cases there was evidence of prior threats to kill. Homicide has far-reaching effects, not just on the family of the victim, but also on the family of the perpetrator, associates of all these people, and officers in the community agencies with whom they are involved, such as police, medical staff, paramedics, members of the judiciary, officers of the court, counsellors, child protection workers and journalists.

There are at least two stories involved in each homicide—the story of the perpetrator and the story of the victim. In addition, the survivors of both the victim and the perpetrator have their stories and their burdens (Allen 1980: 17).

Some countries routinely collect data as part of national homicide monitoring programs, such as the National Homicide Monitoring Program in Australia, the Homicide Survey in Canada, and the Uniform Crime Reports (and Supplementary Homicide Reports) in the United States. This allows us to compare homicide data between countries with reasonable accuracy.

Although the incidence of homicide varies from country to country, the statistics generally remain fairly static over time. Research has shown this is the case in Australia (Mouzos and Rushforth 2003: 33). Australia's homicide rate varied between 1.7 and 2.0 per 100,000 population in the ten years between 1989 and 1999. The total annual number of homicide victims over the decade 1990–99 varied from 297 in 1997–98 to 331 in 1992–93 (Mouzos 2000: 16). In 2001–02 the number of victims climbed to 381, but the rate per 100,000 population remained static at 1.9 (Mouzos and Rushforth 2003: 31–2).

Australian figures are lower than those in the United States of America. There the homicide rate peaked in 1991 at 9.8 per 100,000 population, although it has trended downwards since then, dropping to 5.5 in 2000 (United States Department of Justice 2004). However, the rate of homicide in Australia still exceeds that of England and Wales, and also that of Japan where the rate is 1.1 per 100,000 population (Mouzos 2000: 13).

Causes

Researchers who study homicide categorise it by causal factors, the main ones being 'environmental, sociological, physical and psychological' (Allen 1980: 35). In any particular homicide, the offence is seldom attributable to only one cause; commonly two or more of these factors operate. As Wallace says: 'No single variable analysis can adequately reflect the often complex events and life experiences which culminate in a person taking the life of another, deliberately or otherwise' (1986: 29).

On a per capita basis, homicide generally seems to occur more in cities than in rural areas, and more in impoverished than affluent areas. Allen makes the point that poverty, degradation and humiliation, along with spiritual frustration, 'foster behaviour that reflects the notions that life is cheap and aggression is OK. Violence with some becomes an integrated, acceptable way of life' (Allen 1980: 36).

Conversely, studies of intimate homicide in Australia show that, on a per capita basis, this type of homicide occurs more in rural areas than in cities, whereas homicide generally occurred more or less equally in the city and country over a fourteen-year period. Wallace's study of homicide in New South Wales found 52 per cent of homicides in rural settings involved a victim and offender from the same family. In urban areas only 41 per cent of homicides involved intimates (Wallace 1986: 54). Patricia Easteal, in her comprehensive analysis of Australian spousal homicide, *Killing the Beloved*, records that in Queensland over half of the intimate homicides occurred in the country (1993: 32). Mouzos found that 33 per cent of homicides in Australia in 2000–01 involved family members, with 22 per cent of these classified as having an intimate relationship (2002: 16).

Homicide usually occurs against a backdrop of complex interrelated factors, which are often difficult to unravel after the event. 'Before a murder event occurs, there is usually a build-up in the murderer of many negative, unfulfilling, hopeless, belittling and hostile experiences' (Allen 1980: 37). Poverty and unemployment may be sources of conflict in relationships, and both of these factors are seen to be significant in defining the profile of a perpetrator of homicide. Alcohol is known to be a disinhibitor to violence generally, and to homicide of all types. In this study, although there were reports of various kinds of substance misuse in the perpetrators' histories, it could not be determined from the information available whether or not this was a factor in the offence itself.

In the United States it has been found that race, social class, unemployment, the availability of hand-guns, poverty and alcohol are significant factors in domestic homicide. Cultural differences may be at work here because some of these factors are similar, and some quite different, to Australian data on homicide (Hore, Gibson and Bordow 1996: 5).

The occupational categories of perpetrators vary by country. For instance, Hore and colleagues, in their 1996 study of Australian domestic homicide, refer to Goetting's American study where perpetrators were primarily unemployed. This was slightly different from the findings of Silverman and Mukherjee (1987: 37–47) in Canada and Wallace in New South Wales in 1986. Each of these studies found that the majority of perpetrators were either unskilled or unemployed. In Australia, homicide statistics for 2000–01 show that 65 per cent of perpetrators were unemployed at the time of the offence (Mouzos 2002: 36). Some writers see the threat of loss as being the precursor for male-perpetrated violence, and in extreme cases homicide (Wallace 1986: 123; Polk 1994: 28; Daly and Wilson 1988: 189). So it could be argued that perpetrators who have a greater earning capacity, or who are in possession of greater wealth, are less likely to face loss in terms of either relationships or material resources. However, in my study none of the perpetrators were unskilled or unemployed, although one man was in receipt of an invalid pension.

Physical causes of homicide include alcohol and drug use or abuse, but these are usually disinhibitory, contributory causes that coexist with psychosocial factors. Other contributing physical causes may emanate from genetic influences, or from physiological conditions including 'organic brain disease, brain damage, tumours and temporal lobe epilepsy' (Allen 1980: 38).

It is generally accepted that all crime at a psychological level is the result of interaction between particular constructs of personality, for example, the ego and superego. In the case of homicide, 'The murder event depends on the way these two personality elements have been conditioned by the environment and on the situation to which the person is exposed' (Allen 1980: 42).

It is clear that early experiences, including abandonment, rejection, abuse, and exposure to violence, may damage the formation of both the ego and superego, leaving the individual more vulnerable to stress and less able to integrate the functions of these elements in response to stressors in the environment.

Lack of Individuation in Perpetrator

While working in the Family Court Counselling Service with a number of families where the parents were in serious conflict, I began to notice that men often articulated an inability to regard themselves as an individual, separate from their spouse and children, after marital breakdown. This was associated with problems concerning access, stalking behaviour, and violence against the spouse. A significant number of these men exhibited personality traits consistent with borderline personality disorder (American Psychiatric Association 1994).

Biddulph in *Manhood* discusses the loss of spirituality typically suffered by the majority of men in today's world. He believes this relates to a loss of connectedness which women do not experience in the same way, and that the biggest problem modern man faces is his isolation:

> Falling between the decline of the old ways and the lack of a new 'living' religion, the majority of men just believe in nothing. As a result, they are ill-equipped to answer or handle any of life's deeper questions. Modern man, for all his bravado, is very frail in the face of difficulties. Suicide, cynicism, greed, addiction, wait close beside this path (Biddulph 1994: 193).

If Biddulph is correct in discerning a lack of connectedness and absence of spirituality in today's man, it may indicate that the loss issues at separation could be generally greater for men than for women. In most cases the woman makes the decision to leave, and may have been considering it for some years before the actual separation. The majority of marital separations are initiated by women, and women usually have custody of the children after separating from their spouses, because they are generally the primary care-givers. Suicide following spousal homicide, where the couple are separated, occurs twice as often as when the couple are still living together (Easteal 1993: 103). This raises the question of whether the man is able to maintain his denial of the loss of the relationship as long as his wife remains physically at his side. It could be speculated that once she leaves the home, he is forced to acknowledge the loss of the relationship. All the couples in this study were living separately at the time of the offence.

Perpetrator Intention

Whereas some researchers have categorised homicide by the inter-relationship of causal factors, Allen categorises it using concepts of perpetrator intent. These were developed by E. S. Schneidman (1976: 6), an eminent researcher whose study of suicide event focused on 'the role of the individual in his own demise'. Allen adapts Schneidman's concepts to describe three types of homicide:

- intentional: the perpetrator has a conscious intention to kill the victim
- sub-intentional: the victim has a major role in their own demise, for instance by self-destructive, violent, abusive or risk-taking behaviour
- unintentional: the victim plays no role in their own demise but is simply in the wrong place at the wrong time (1980: 47).

> Concerning sub-intentional homicide, Easteal notes:
>
> Sub-intentional homicide or victim precipitation, the way in which the victim's actions, or behaviours, prior to the homicide, contributed to the death, remains a problematic concept in intimate homicide, as it is a 'subjective assessment by the investigator', made often on the basis of the perpetrator's interpretation of the event (1993: 5).

Constructs Present in Homicidal Incidents

Allen describes four constructs she considers to be present in all homicidal incidents. Again these constructs are adapted from Schneidman's (1976) earlier work on suicide:

1   Inimicality, which refers to the 'self-antagonistic parts' of an individual's character that have their roots in early life. These aspects of self are reinforced by aversive life experiences, and may be either turned outwards aggressively towards the other, or focused inwards against the self in some form of self-destructive behaviour. In extreme cases this interplay of intra-psychic and environmental factors can lead to homicidal or suicidal behaviour.

2   Perturbation, a negative emotional state that is a consequence of a range of physical, psychological and sociological influences. It consists of turmoil, agitation, and restlessness, and is a state of extreme stress. When it combines with powerlessness and inimicality in an individual, the risk of violence is increased significantly and leads to constriction.

3   Constriction is a narrowing of one's world view and a lack of awareness of options. The person is unable to make positive associations and there is a lack of feeling of responsibility. The person is preoccupied with their own distress, and murder appears to be the only solution to the problem they are experiencing.

4   Cessation: the perpetrator decides that the permanent removal (cessation) of the person perceived to be the 'cause' of the problem is the only solution to the stress being experienced. Then homicide is likely (Allen 1980: 48–9).

These constructs, described by Allen as being generally present in homicidal incidents, may be readily applied to spousal homicide and familicide. Both these kinds of offences tend to occur where emotionally inadequate individuals are faced with a major life crisis, such as separation or divorce from their partner and estrangement from their children, without having the psychosocial resources to deal with the resultant suffering.

Characteristics of Homicide Perpetrators

It is generally accepted that perpetrators of homicide have an inability to manage their impulses, or have an under-developed superego. In most cases it has been found they come from socially and economically disadvantaged families, and have experienced an upbringing characterised by emotional deprivation and/or violence (Lunde 1975: 96). As violence is a learned behaviour, it is likely that 'children exposed to the regularity of violence at an early and impressionable age, learn (are conditioned to the idea) that killing is an acceptable way of resolving conflict' (Allen 1980: 44).

Homicide as a Social Act

Early research on homicide focused on the characteristics of victims or offenders. In 1958 there was a change in direction when Wolfgang in *Patterns of Criminal Homicide* proposed that the relationship between the victim and the offender should be considered within the context of the homicide event. In his view:

> homicide is a dynamic relationship between two or more persons caught up in a life drama where they operate in a direct, interactional relationship. More so than in any other violation of conduct norms, the relationship the victim bears to the offender plays a role in explaining the reasons for such flagrant violation (Wolfgang 1958: 203).

Wolfgang expanded on this by examining the closeness of the relationship between the perpetrator and the victim, thereby dispelling any myth which might have existed about homicide usually taking place between strangers.

> Homicide is most likely to occur where some form of close relationship exists. In fact, of the homicides that occur where the victim and offender are known to one another, the most common relationship is that of family member (1958: 4).

It is now recognised that homicide is 'fundamentally a social act, and therefore it is important to explore the relationships that exist among the key actors in the event' (Polk 1994: 3). Research confirms that homicide more commonly occurs where the victim is known to the offender than where the victim and offender are strangers (Wallace 1986; Strang 1991, 1993; Easteal 1993; Polk 1994; Hore, Gibson and Bordow 1996; Mouzos and Rushforth 2003).

Gender

Research conducted in Australia and abroad indicates that the majority of homicide offenders are male. In most studies, the proportion of male to female offenders is approximately four to one (Curtis 1974, cited in Wallace 1986: 29; Mouzos and Rushforth 2003: 42–3).

Wallace's study of homicide in New South Wales between 1968 and 1981 showed that the proportion of male perpetrators there was higher, at five to six males for each female offender. She also refers to data from South Australia, where the Office of Crime Statistics Report for 1981 showed an even higher proportion of male offenders, at ten males to each female (1986: 29). In 2000–01, Australian homicide statistics show the ratio was closer to eight males to one female offender (Mouzos 2002: 35). It is not clear why more Australian men commit homicide, as compared to women, than in most other countries. It is likely that the explanation will be found in a complex inter-relationship of socio-cultural factors.

In Australia in 1989–90 there were 215 male victims of homicide and 114 female victims (Strang 1991: 23). In 2000–01 there were 192 male victims of homicide and 125 female victims (Mouzos 2002: 28). This indicates that, in Australia, men have a significantly higher risk than women of becoming a homicide victim.

Offender–Victim Groups

Of all victims, whether adult or child, 83 per cent of male victims were killed by men, and 90 per cent of female victims were killed by men. Where the victim was an adult (aged over sixteen years) the chance of the offender being male was greater: 86 per cent for male victims and 97 per cent for female victims (Wallace 1986: 71). Furthermore, Mouzos (1999a: 11) in her nine-year Australian study found that where men are most likely to be killed by a friend or acquaintance (45 per cent), women are more likely to be murdered by their intimate partner (60 per cent).

Although most homicides in Wallace's 1986 study were committed by males against males (53 per cent), the second most common category of homicide was committed by males against females (32.5 per cent). A total of 85 per cent of all homicide offenders in this study were males, leaving 15 per cent female offenders. More recent statistics show that this trend has not changed significantly, with 89 per cent of homicide offenders being male and only 11 per cent female (Mouzos 2002: 15).

Victim–Offender Relationship

It is widely accepted that women are most at risk of violence, including homicide, from their sexual partner. 'Overall, on average, every six hours an American woman is killed by her husband or boyfriend' (Levine et al., cited in Ewing 1987: 5).

In a study of all homicides that took place in the city of Detroit in 1972, 127 or one-quarter of the total number of victims had a relationship with their murderer, and 80 of these were in a spousal relationship with their murderer (Daly and Wilson 1988: 4). More recent statistics from the United States, between 1976 and 2000, show that most homicide victims were familiar with their assailant, that 11 per cent of all homicide victims were killed by an intimate, and that one-third of female murder victims were killed by an intimate, whereas only 4 per cent of male murder victims are killed by an intimate (United States Department of Justice 2002).

At the time my study commenced, the precise relationship between offender and victim was not always noted in Australian homicide records, although each jurisdiction had a category to record family relationships. The degree to which this category was broken down depended upon the jurisdiction in which the offence occurred, and the purpose for which the data was sought. (Information provided by the Crime Information Unit, Western Australian Police Department 1996.)

Strang found that, in Australia, 21 per cent of homicides took place between spouses, and that socio-economic class and gender are two 'major social vectors that run through homicide data' (1993: 5). In other words, a small percentage of offenders are women and a small percentage are highly educated. This profile correlates with what is known about violence generally: males are more likely to perpetrate violence than women. Although Strang could determine the employment status of offenders in only two-thirds of cases, less than one-third of these was in the paid workforce at the time of the offence (1993: 29–30).

In Victoria, Naylor and Neale have shown that

> between 1948 and 1975, 52% of homicides committed in that state fell into the 'Special Relationships' category. This category used by the police to define victim–offender relationships includes family relationships, lovers, and is used to describe victim–offender relationships in situations where a family relationship appeared to have precipitated the killing. This category is slightly wider than the 'family relationships' category used in the previously cited New South Wales study, but it captures the essential idea of the domestic homicide (1988: 2).

(Since Naylor and Neale's study, this category has been revised to define the victim–offender relationship more clearly, bringing it into line with other jurisdictions.)

In a separate study of Victorian homicide, 1985–89, Polk found that of 380 homicides, 101 occurred within the context of sexual intimacy, and another 40 originated in family intimacy. Of the 101 murders of sexual intimates, in 86 situations the offender was male, and in 73 of these 86 cases the victim was the female partner of the offender. Interestingly, although most of the female killings were the result of the male using violence to assert his control over her, there were 15 cases where the male was assessed to be severely depressed and the homicide appeared to be part of the planned suicide of the male (Polk 1994: 24). Polk concludes:

> There appear to be two distinct major sub-patterns to the homicide where men kill women, one concerned with sexual possession where violence is employed as a control strategy, the other with a

pattern of suicidal masculine depression which also encompasses the female partner in a control process, but to quite a different end (1994: 28).

In one of the cases Polk studied, it was reported that, prior to the offence, the man had behaved so unusually towards his daughter that she had considered the possibility of him committing suicide (1994: 48).

Spousal Homicide

Durkheim noted that, although family life tends to have a moderating effect on suicide, it seems to increase the risk of homicide. In a general sense, the obligations and rights of marriage at the time he wrote were seen to favour men, and therefore Durkheim suggested that when a marriage ended, the man in effect had more to lose (Durkheim 1968: 188–9, 354, 384–5).

In Australia spousal homicide, like homicide generally, is an offence primarily committed by men. Some early theorists proposed that male violence, of which homicide is the most extreme form, is biologically based and that male aggressiveness was a result of the male role in most societies to 'impregnate women, protect dependants from danger, and provision kith and kin' (Gilmore 1990: 223, cited in Polk 1994: 203). More recent research emphasises the interplay between environmental, sociological, and psychological phenomena in attempting to understand causal factors. As the majority of homicide victims and perpetrators are known to have had a social relationship of some kind before the offence, it is also important to find out the nature and extent of that relationship in attempting to hypothesise about cause.

In Wallace's study, four out of five victims knew the offender. Most relationships were recorded as being close and took place within the context of 'family' (1986: 93).

Some writers argue that the victimisation of women and children in our society is a result of the sexist structure of our social environment. They take the position that because males have a superior position in terms of power, women tend to 'make themselves subservient to men'.

Children are even less powerful than women, are usually primarily cared for by women, and economically, through their mothers, are dependent on men. This, the argument goes, leads men to assume a proprietary attitude towards their wives and children, and perceived failure on the woman's part to adhere to principles of loyalty and fidelity is met with violence (Gates 1978: 11).

Anglo-American law is replete with examples of men's proprietary entitlements over the sexuality and reproductive capacity of wives and daughters. Since before the time of William the Conqueror there has been a continual elaboration of legal devices enabling men to seek monetary redress for the theft and damage of their women's sexuality and reproductive capacity (Wilson and Daly 1992: 85).

Becker and Abel examine the various forms that victimisation of women takes, taking a strongly feminist perspective:

A variety of social, legal, and psychological forms of victimisation are perpetrated by men on women. We live in a society in which men are in charge of the majority of institutions. Economically, women are discriminated against in the job market. Sex role stereotyping has victimised and 'imprisoned' a number of women. Often women have been victimised by the institution of marriage, in which, although they are no longer identified as property, they are still repressed by implied and covert social-cultural practices. In some cases in the course of a marital relationship, women have been exploited physically, emotionally and sexually by their husbands (1978: 29).

In spousal homicide, male perpetrators generally outnumber females by at least three to one. Spousal homicide is usually preceded by a history of physical violence inflicted by the male partner on the female, so it is likely that there is an inherent imbalance of power between the parties. The Marxist feminist perspective is:

a gender-based division of labour arises in class, and especially in capitalist societies, by which males provide subsistence for their wives and children, results in extensive economic dependency of women on men. It is unequal economic power, rooted primarily in the behaviour of economic elites, that explains gender stratification from this perspective (Chafetz 1988: 63).

From a Marxist feminist perspective then, this gender inequality may lead society to view women as socially inferior to men, and cause some men to view women as chattels or wards rather than as equal partners. Within this theoretical framework, men may not see that women have the right to terminate a relationship either by infidelity or by leaving. As society assigns little value to women's domestic work, women often suffer from low self-esteem and when they find themselves in abusive relationships they feel powerless to extricate themselves. When they do attempt to leave they often suffer from economic hardship and lack of community support (Women's Coalition Against Family Violence 1994: 35–6).

In the United Kingdom in a ten-year period from 1972 to 1982, between 21 and 29 per cent of all homicide victims were spouses or ex-spouses killed by their partners (Edwards 1985, cited in Easteal 1993: 2). In Canada for the same period, the proportion was higher. Homicide statistics from three Canadian cities 1976–82 showed that, while 75 per cent of all killings 'involved people with some level of intimacy, 41 per cent involved either those currently or once married or in de facto relationships' (Silverman and Mukherjee 1987: 42–3). In Australia in 1992–93, 'For about a third of homicides where the relationship was recorded, the relationship was spousal or between other family members: Nearly two-thirds of these family murders were between spouses' (Strang 1993: 1). In Australia between 1989 and 1996, over 25 per cent of all homicides which occurred where the offender was known involved intimate partners (Carcach and James 1998: 1).

Very nearly one quarter (23.2%) of all homicides in New South Wales occurred between spouses, with three times as many men killing their wives as there were wives killing husbands. Women were particularly vulnerable in spouse homicides: almost half (47%) of all female victims were killed by their spouse compared with only 10% of the male victims (Naylor and Neale 1988: 83).

More recently Mouzos reported that only 11 per cent of adult male victims were killed by their intimate partners, compared to 61 per cent of adult female victims (2000: 115).

It is acknowledged that males more frequently respond to separation with homicidal violence than females do (Wilson and Daly 1992: 89–93). In addition:

– Men are more likely than women to hunt down and kill spouses who have left them.
– Men are more likely than women to kill a partner as part of a planned murder–suicide.
– Men kill in response to revelations of their wife's infidelity; women almost never respond similarly, although men are more often unfaithful.
– Some men kill their wives after subjecting them to long periods of violence; some women kill male partners after suffering years of physical violence, after they have exhausted all avenues of assistance, feel trapped, fear for their lives or those of their children.
– Men commit familicidal massacres, killing spouse and children together; women do not.
– A large proportion of spousal killings perpetrated by wives, but almost none of those perpetrated by husbands, are acts of self-defence (Wilson and Daly 1992, cited in Hore, Gibson and Bordow 1996: 10).

Polk asserts that it is important to gain understanding of the conflict preceding homicide in order to better understand homicidal events (1994: 22). He refers to two major themes in homicide where men kill women. The first is concerned with masculine sexual possession, where 'violence is employed as a control strategy' (1994: 28). He

refers to Rasche's 1989 study, which found that 'the single most important motive for murder among intimates was the inability of the
offender to accept the termination of the relationship' (Rasche 1989,
cited in Polk 1994: 28). In these cases it is postulated that the primary
aim is the destruction (homicide) of the woman. Those cases where this
occurred are explained thus: 'the powerful motives of jealousy and loss
of control resulted in the male taking his own life as well as that of his
sexual partner' (Polk 1994: 44). Polk's analysis is useful in teasing out
the complex and critical factors in the dynamics of spousal homicide,
but it does not answer the underlying question as to why jealousy and
loss of control motivate the perpetrator's suicide; neither does it explain
why suicide occurs in some of this type of spousal homicide by men and
yet not in others.

The second theme in spousal homicide by men is of 'masculine
suicidal depression resulting from a depressive crisis which also encompasses the female partner in a control process but to quite a different
end'. Polk asserts that these men 'reach the point of insisting, after they
have concluded that their own lives must end, that their partner should
be a part of this decision as well' (1994: 44). He postulates that these
cases vary from the first type because the primary aim is the suicide of
the perpetrator. Interestingly, Polk reports that there was no indication
of jealousy in this pattern of spousal homicide.

SUICIDE

Pritchard (1995: 90) notes that Durkheim in *Le Suicide*, published in
1888, found that the causes of suicide are of two types, which he defines
as 'organic psychic dispositions' and the 'nature of the physical environment'. Pritchard explains that individuals are largely defined in terms of
their social relationships, and that divorce precipitates some level of
isolation that can cause them to feel stigmatised and socially rejected.
He reports that Durkheim had noted the association of divorce and
suicide in nineteenth-century Europe (Pritchard 1995: 59, 91).

In Australia, the leading cause of death among men between the
ages of twenty-five and forty-four is self-inflicted death. According to
Australian Bureau of Statistics data on causes of death in 2002, suicide

accounted for 31 deaths per 100,000 males aged twenty-five to twenty-nine, and almost 31 deaths per 100,000 males aged thirty to thirty-four (Australian Bureau of Statistics 2002b).

Steve Biddulph, the well-known champion of males in Western urbanised society, asserts that 'Men and boys commit suicide four times more frequently than women' (1994: 6). He seems to be quoting figures that apply only to Australia, but this is not certain.

Murder–Suicide

A certain percentage of murders are followed by the suicide of the perpetrator. This is more common when the relationship between victim and offender is known to have been close, as in the case of spousal homicide.

In Wallace's fourteen-year New South Wales study, approximately one in fifty-six suicides was accompanied by homicide, and one in ten homicides was coupled with a suicide. Thus of 1373 homicides, 144 were followed by the suicide of the perpetrator, and a further 44 killings were accompanied by an unsuccessful suicide attempt. Therefore, in total, one in seven homicides could properly be classified as suicide–murder. It was frequently a matter of chance that a suicide attempt failed—in most cases there was no evidence of any qualitative distinction (in terms of motivation) between successful and unsuccessful suicides (Wallace 1986: 157).

Daly and Wilson report that remorseful suicide following murder is rare. They found that in over six and a half thousand Canadian homicides, 'there were just 8 killers who committed suicide after a delay that might reflect remorseful brooding' (1988: 217).

Spousal Murder Followed by Suicide

> Suicidal killers are mainly men who have killed women, and more particularly women with whom they have (or in some cases only aspire to) a sexual relationship (Daly and Wilson 1988: 217).

Spousal homicide is almost always preceded by years of physical abuse and a gross imbalance of power in the relationship between the parties. A study of femicide in Australia between 1880 and 1939 found that with the onset of the twentieth century there was an increase in femicide of women who ended violent relationships by leaving: 'the women's desertion or threat to desert because of violence precipitated the violent attack'. However, then as now, it appeared that women deserted by their male partners did not behave in this way: 'In marked contrast, women did not pursue and physically attack spouses who deserted them' (O'Donnell and Craney 1982: 5).

Daly and Wilson found that, in Canada in the period 1974–83, men killed 786 spouses without also killing their children, whereas women killed only 248 spouses without also killing their children. During this period, twenty-six men killed their spouse and children, but no women committed this type of offence. Over the twenty-three years 1961 to 1984 in Canada, there were sixty-one cases of familicide 'in which a Canadian man killed his wife and one or more children', but there was 'not a single such massacre by a wife' (Daly and Wilson 1988: 82–3).

> In every society for which we have been able to find a sample of spousal homicides, the story is basically the same: Most cases arise out of the husband's jealous, proprietary, violent response to his wife's (real or imagined) infidelity or desertion (Daly and Wilson 1988: 202).

A significant number of spousal and family killings are followed by the suicide of the perpetrator (West 1965: 1; Wallace 1986: 96; Strang 1993: 33; Carcach and Grabosky 1998: 3). For homicides committed in Australia in 1991–92, Strang reports that nineteen of the perpetrators committed suicide after the offence (eighteen of them were men) and another six attempted suicide (1993: 33). In most of these cases, the perpetrator and victim had been in a spousal or other family relationship.

Interestingly, suicide following spousal homicide when the couple are separated is twice as common as when the couple are still living together (Easteal 1993: 103). This raises questions about the psychology of the perpetrator and the presence of depression or other mental illness. It may be that a lack of individuation makes the separation unbearable to the perpetrator and that the murder–suicide is in fact (from an intra-psychic perspective) a suicide–suicide. This may explain why it has been reported in the literature that the characteristics of some familicides, particularly where men kill their families, are more consistent with suicide than with homicide (West 1965: 175). In this study all couples were separated.

Polk notes that perpetrators appear to have different motivations in spousal homicide. In cases where the man murdered his partner out of a sense of possessive jealousy and then suicided, the primary motivation seems to have been the murder of the woman. In cases where the man was suffering depression, his primary motivation seems to have been suicide, 'but a similar sense of possessiveness, decreed that they should take their wives with them rather than leave them behind' (1994: 48, 49).

> [In cases] where the homicide is part of the male suicide plan the woman is clearly seen as a possession, or commodity, which the man must dispose of prior to his own death. In these cases as well, the killing represents the ultimate control of the man over the woman (there were no cases where a depressed woman killed her male partner as part of her suicide plan) (Polk 1994: 57).

Child Homicide Including Filicide

Children comprise between 10 and 20 per cent of homicide victims in Australia, the United Kingdom and North America (Alder and Polk 2001). Wallace found that child killing or filicide is most often an unpremeditated crime undertaken in haste. It is rare for this offence to involve more than one victim (1986: 116). A 1995 Australian study reported that only 9 per cent of child murders included more than one child (NSW CPC 1995, cited in Wilczynski 1997: 86).

> This study indicated that children under one year old are usually at highest risk of being murdered by their parents, with mothers

being more likely than fathers to kill their children. In the same study, twenty-one per cent of victims (including multiple victims) were aged under one year, and forty-two per cent were aged between 1– 4 years (Wilczynski 1997: 87).

In Wallace's New South Wales study, 27 per cent of suspected perpetrators were found to have attempted suicide following their offence, and 22 per cent were successful (1986: 93).

Wilson asserts that in order to truly interpret the patterns in child killing, one needs to see violence against children, including child homicide, in a historical, social and cultural context rather than simply considering statistics.

In a sense, our outrage and horror at the murder of children is at once understandable and hypocritical. It is understandable because the killing of a child violates, in a dramatic and symbolic way, all that we have been taught about protecting our children and the innocence within them that we are supposed to preserve. It is hypocritical because children are not, and never have been, accorded the legal and social protections that we suggest they should have (Wilson 1985: 25–6).

Wallace's study of New South Wales reported that 68 per cent of child homicide victims (those aged under sixteen years) were aged five years or less, and that 83 per cent were killed by a parent (1986: 112).

Wilczynski categorised child homicide according to the perpetrator's motivation (1997: 44). Categories used to record this relationship vary, and this must be borne in mind when comparing studies by different researchers. Wilczynski names one category 'Retaliating', in which anger towards the perpetrator's sexual partner is displaced onto the child victim. Another term for this type of killing is 'spouse revenge' (Resnick 1969, cited in Wilczynski 1997: 45). Wilczynski found, as did Daly and Wilson (1988: 213–19), that men were far more likely to commit retaliatory killings than women. Polk, commenting on Wallace's study, reports that after deaths by traumatic injury (child abuse) numbering thirteen, the next largest group of child victims were those killed as part of their parent's suicide, these cases numbering nine (Polk 1994: 25). Wallace concluded that in these cases the parent was motivated by a concern for the welfare of the child, although this was not grounded in rational thought because of the parent's emotional state at the time.

> Altruistic intentions appeared to motivate the offenders to take the lives of the children when they suicided—altruistic in the sense that regard for the well-being of the child was a primary concern. However, none of these cases could be called mercy killings—there was no evidence to suggest any real degree of suffering in the victim. The primary feature was considered to be overwhelming depression and mental anguish on the part of the offender rather than any hostility toward the victim. The interpretation is that for various reasons, largely unrelated to the children, e.g., financial, health or emotional problems, the parents contemplated suicide. But they could not face leaving their dependants behind, defenceless and unprotected (in their view) to face the world alone (Wallace 1986: 132).

Wallace studied cases where the offence was murder followed by suicide; she showed that suicidal women kill their children, but not their partners, before they suicide. Other writers hypothesise that because of violence, child abuse or other factors, the woman may be attempting to escape from the male partner and rescue her children from him (Daly and Wilson 1988: 216). Men, however, tend to kill both their wives and their children before taking their own lives. Wallace comments on the lack of individuation in these offenders:

> A typical feature of these murder–suicides was that the offender did not appear to regard his/her victim as having a separate personality with an independent right to life. Rather, the victim was regarded as being an extension of the offender, sharing their troubles and to be taken with them into death (Wallace 1986: 132).

In their recent book on child homicide, Alder and Polk refer to the work of Daly and Wilson, which showed that 'filicidal genetic parents of both sexes are often deeply depressed, are likely to kill their children while they sleep, and may even construe murder–suicide as a humane act of rescue from a cruel world'. Daly and Wilson are also reported to have found that homicidal step-parents rarely suicide (Daly and Wilson 1998, cited in Alder and Polk 2001: 149).

Alder and Polk's study of child homicide in Victoria found that the proportion of women offenders was higher than among homicide offenders in general, but the incidence of male perpetrators was still marginally higher. Only nine of the twenty-three male perpetrators were the biological father of the child; in most cases the male was the de facto partner of the child's mother (2001: 68).

Alder and Polk refer to the level of premeditation which takes place in some familicides, and comment on the difference in perpetrator mood between this type of offence and many child homicides which are not followed by suicide. 'Emotions of extreme despair and hopelessness, or determination and commitment, run through some of these events rather than, or as well as, fury and rage' (2001: 153–4).

Familicide

The majority of intimate homicides (95 per cent) consist of a single perpetrator and a single victim (Easteal 1993: 35–6). A small number have multiple victims, and even more of these crimes culminate in the suicide, or attempted suicide, of the perpetrator than in spousal homicide. These cases of multiple homicide followed by suicide of the perpetrator are called 'familicide' in the small amount of literature on this topic. In 14 per cent of murder–suicides in Australia, a parent kills their children before suiciding. In an additional 6 per cent, a parent kills both their partner and their children before suiciding (Carcach and Grabosky 1998: 3).

Cases of familicide make 'A substantial contribution to the murder rate, since murders are counted by the number of bodies' (West 1965: 1). I could not find separate statistics for this offence. Familicide is occasionally mentioned in the literature relating to spousal homicide, but the term is rarely used in general texts on homicide. Therefore, information must be gleaned from other writings on homicide, particularly from case studies.

Alder and Polk found that when a biological father kills his children, it is often where the couple is separated or where the man believes that separation is likely to occur (2001: 87). This is consistent with the findings of other researchers in the area, and only one child in my study was not the biological child of the perpetrator.

Wallace (1986), Easteal (1993), Polk (1994), Wilczynski (1997) and other writers have discussed various theoretical propositions relevant to understanding the motivation for familicide committed by men. One is that the perpetrator is motivated by a need to retaliate against his spouse for her desertion of him by killing her and/or the children. Another is that the marital separation precipitates a deep depression in the perpetrator that causes him to include his children, and possibly his spouse, in his suicidal ideation. A third is that the man's pssessiveness and obsessive need to control the victims leads to homicide. We will look at these three propositions.

Retaliatory Familicide

Retaliatory killing of a child, or spouse revenge, usually occurs when anger towards the perpetrator's sexual partner is displaced onto the child (d'Orban, cited in Wilczynski 1997: 45).

This may explain cases where the children are killed and the wife is not. The homicide may be retaliatory, and although there may have been threats to kill her, the wife is allowed to survive to experience the pain of living without her children. Her suffering will be intensified by her knowledge that it was her 'desertion' of the husband which 'caused' the loss of her offspring. It could be said that the husband is paying his wife back for leaving him and taking the children, by 'leaving' her and taking the children as well, in an act that far exceeds hers both in the level of violence and in its finality.

A recent Victorian study found these offences were characterised by 'feelings of jealousy, anger and rage'. In several cases the evidence seemed to indicate that vindictiveness towards the mother of the children was part of the offender's motive. In addition it was noted that, 'The most powerful motivating factors seem to be in relation to harming and establishing ultimate control over the wife' (Alder and Polk 2001: 78–83).

Familicide Caused by Suicidal Masculine Depression

Interestingly, Alder and Polk found that 'most of the mothers who committed filicide–suicide had at some point sought psychiatric treatment, but this was not the case for the men' (2001: 84). It is well known that men are less likely to seek help for emotional problems than women are. For some men the feelings elicited by the loss, or perceived loss, of their partner and children are so extreme that they cannot cope; thus suicide becomes a method of resolving their suffering. This, however, does not explain the murder of their children or acts of violence towards their wives.

As described previously in relation to spousal killings, some cases of familicide more closely resemble suicide rather than homicide. When children are killed in this type of homicide, it is suggested that the proprietary attitude of the male gives him permission to include the children in what is intended principally as his own suicide (Ewing 1997: 133–5).

Easteal found that, although homicide offences that occur between adult sexual intimates and involve multiple victims are rare, those that do are likely to also include the suicide of the offender. She found that, in Australia in 1989–90 and 1990–92, of the seven intimate homicide incidents that involved more than one victim, in six cases the killer committed suicide. She interpreted the suicide of the offender in these cases as indicating remorse. 'As most of these other victims were children, again the argument about remorse as motivator gains strength' (1993: 97).

Another explanation comes from Carcach and Grabosky (1998: 4, referring to Henry and Short, cited in Stack 1997). They 'argue that perpetrators of murder–suicide are trapped in the frustration–nurturance–frustration cycle'. This proposition may fit spousal homicide–suicide, but it does not seem to be relevant for explaining child murder followed by suicide. Carcach and Grabosky propose that the suicide component of these offences represents aggression focused on the self, as a result of the homicide-induced frustration at the loss of the source of nurturance (1998: 4). This provides a possible explanation of spousal homicide–suicide, especially in those cases where a firearm is used in rage and haste. However, it does not explain cases where there is evidence of premeditation, and therefore it does not readily fit filicide–suicide, which characteristically shows significant elements of premeditation. The premeditation includes the perpetrator as victim, so this would appear to exclude the explanation that the suicide component of these offences (from a psychological perspective) is a separate event occurring as a result of the homicide.

It seems much more likely that the perpetrator's lack of individuation from the children and the spouse leads to homicide as an extension of the perpetrator's suicide. Many cases display characteristics that are more consistent with suicide than with homicide, such as the existence of premeditation, the leaving of notes, and perpetrator depression. In some of these cases the antecedents point towards a retaliatory motive, so that the perpetrator sees the homicide–suicide as a way of obtaining revenge on his partner for leaving the relationship.

Familicide and Masculine Possessiveness

The third proposition relevant to familicide is that possessiveness, and an obsessive need to control partner and children, causes perpetrators to respond violently in response to the threat of separation and the feelings of jealousy precipitated by this (Daly and Wilson 1988 cited in Polk 1994: 28). The motivation in these cases arises from the proprietary attitude of: 'If I can't have them no-one will'. All respondents in this study described the men as having proprietary attitudes towards their families and of refusing to accept separation, thus masculine possession was a factor in these offences. What is not clear is why none of the women were killed along with the children. Masculine possession would also appear to be a factor in familicides characterised by suicidal masculine depression, in that the man's perception of ownership apparently gives him the right to kill his spouse and/or his children in conjunction, or as part of, his own suicide. Again, the issue of lack of individuation of the perpetrator seems relevant in considering the intra-psychic processes and motivation of these men, when they plan and execute these very premeditated offences.

SUMMARY

The literature review highlighted the paucity of information in relation to familicide. Many of the homicide texts used the same major references, some of which are now dated. The literature on spousal homicide–suicide and filicide was the most relevant to this study. Regarding the motivation of the perpetrator, Polk's conceptualisation of it in spousal homicide as having themes of either 'masculine possession' or 'masculine depression' (1994: 27–57), and Wilczynski's conceptualisation of it in filicide as being 'retaliating' (1997: 45), appear to be highly relevant. However, given that aspects of these conditions appear to coexist in some perpetrators who are the subject of this study, it is clear that these concepts alone do not explain familicide, and that much more research is needed before the offence can be truly understood. An important area for future examination is the intra-psychic functioning of the perpetrator before the offence. Understanding is most likely to come from a blend of criminological, sociological and psychological theorising.

CHAPTER — 8

Keeping Children Safe

Men are hurting. They are also hurting others. Physical violence against spouses, and a horrific incidence of child sexual abuse, points to something badly wrong with large numbers of men. Then there is the stuff of front page news: sexual abductions and murders of women and children, shopping mall massacres and the like. Men, always men (Biddulph 1994: 2).

My study aimed to isolate common factors in familicide in order to increase understanding of why these offences occur.

The primary finding is that there are significant commonalities in familicide offences where there was an apparent dispute about custody of, or access to, the children. Domestic violence was present in every case where details of the spousal relationship were known. The men were characterised by obsessiveness, lack of individuation and pathological jealousy, including jealousy of their own children. Egocentricity and threats to harm self and others were common. Most of these characteristics were universally present where detailed information about the nature of family relationships was accessible. Before the offence, there were obvious signs in the man's behaviour indicating a deterioration in his mental health, which in turn affected his ability to cope with the separation. Apparently none of the men (with one possible exception) sought treatment for their mental illness, but I could not verify this because most of them had committed suicide.

Although the research does not indicate any direct relationship between familicide and disputed custody and access, it does suggest a strong link between familicide and fear of abandonment or loss of control. It seems likely from the data that a dispute about custody and access could have been another manifestation of the perpetrator's inability to separate from, or relinquish control of, his partner and children. It is of particular interest that none of the survivors interviewed in this study had perceived that there was a dispute with the perpetrator in relation to custody or access at the time of the offence. There was no indication, from the data available, that any of the men had been prevented from having contact with their children. Where information was available about the nature of the perpetrator's family relationships, there were indications that the man held a proprietary view of his wife and children, that this had existed before the separation, and that it had contributed to the breakdown of the couple's relationship.

FAMILICIDE AND OTHER FORMS OF FAMILY HOMICIDE

There were four significant differences between factors associated with the offences studied and those that usually accompany spousal homicide and filicide.

Firstly, in all but one case the victims were the biological children of the perpetrator; in most child homicides committed by a male in the family setting, the victims are stepchildren or children of a de facto partner. Secondly, the occupational status of the perpetrator was higher than that usually found in spousal homicide or other child homicide.

Thirdly, the venue of the offence (except for one case) was public open space, whereas child homicide is usually committed in the family home. Finally, the cause of death in both victims and perpetrators differed significantly from the Australian norm. As we saw in Chapter 1, in most child homicides the cause of death is manual assault, and in male suicides the cause of death is usually hanging or strangulation. The principal cause of death for most victims in this study was carbon monoxide poisoning.

Despite threats of spousal homicide in a number of cases, it appears there was only one case where the man tried to kill his ex-partner at the same time as he killed the children. This cannot be verified as his motive could not be determined.

DISPELLING MYTHS

The conclusions of the study show that there are common themes in these offences, but misconceptions still exist in the community about causal factors.

For example, the press on occasions depicts familicide as an act of love rather than an act of extreme and premeditated violence. Although there were reports that some of the men demonstrated love for their children and were involved in their care, in most cases they had shown little interest in child-rearing or the day-to-day care of the children before the separation.

Another misconception is that familicide is caused by a legal dispute. In this study only one couple had a current dispute in the court. Yet another commonly held belief is that familicide is caused by the man's lack of contact with his children, but in six of these cases the man had contact and used his time with the children to kill them. In the case where the man did not kill his children during access but shot them while they slept, he had consistently refused to exercise access although encouraged and supported to do so by his ex-wife.

DOMESTIC VIOLENCE

Domestic violence was under-reported to the courts and to the police by female victims. The effect on children of witnessing violence and other forms of abuse was almost ignored by women and their legal representatives. Where violence was reported to the court, it did not always influence the court's perception of the risk posed to children by contact with the perpetrator. Where the court possessed information relating to a perpetrator's previous violence, apparently it was not available to decision-makers.

TRAUMA EFFECTS

The interviews confirmed that the trauma of familicide is enduring and far-reaching, not simply for survivors in the immediate family but also for the extended family and friends. The women also commented that professionals involved with them appeared to suffer what is now referred to as vicarious trauma (Saakvitne and Pearlman 1996: 17).

Respondents reported major changes in the functioning of family members, including themselves, after the offence. Examples included the onset of mental illness, altered attitudes towards children and towards males, changed child-rearing practices, and substance abuse.

The respondents' suffering was intense, as one would expect. It is known that trauma can affect perceptions of the trauma event itself, and may affect the functioning of individuals long after the event. Survivors were not assessed for their levels of post-traumatic stress or for the existence of post-traumatic stress disorder, although they often reported symptoms of the latter.

In addition to these significant common factors, all the offences studied incorporate at least one of three homicide–suicide characteristics. Firstly, there was evidence of the characteristics of retaliatory homicide followed by suicide. Here the prime motive appears to be revenge upon the spouse by killing the child or children; lack of individuation from the spouse, and consequential inability to survive the separation, may explain the suicidal component of the offence.

Secondly, in other cases there was evidence characteristic of a depression-driven suicide, where the man appears to lack individuation from both his partner and his children, and sees no future for himself or the children outside the original family unit. The homicide component appears to emanate from the man's inability to conceptualise his children as having an existence separate from his own. They become victims, by extension, of his own suicide.

Finally some cases evidenced possessiveness and obsessive control by the perpetrator linked to his inability to conceptualise and accept separation.

All the offences researched appear to have characteristics of one or other of these categories, but some appear to have characteristics of more than one. It is not clear from the available evidence why this should be the case. Until follow-up research is undertaken with surviving perpetrators, their motivation remains a matter of conjecture.

TOWARDS UNDERSTANDING

This study was an exploratory project, and was not intended to answer hypotheses but only to map the subject area with a view to generating hypotheses, and point the way for future research in this neglected area.

The study is limited by the small number of cases examined, even though it comprises all the familicides in Western Australia during the given period where disputed custody or access was a factor. However, the relatively low incidence of such offences and the richness of the data gained from the collective case study approach is believed to justify it.

It would have been advantageous to interview surviving perpetrators of attempted familicides or their families, as this would undoubtedly have provided a different perspective on the offences. Clearly, more research is needed to explore the experiences of paternal families, including those of any surviving perpetrators. The difficulty of locating these families and persuading them to share their experiences makes them worthy of a separate study.

By linking the knowledge of how individuals cope with loss to research on borderline personality disorder (American Psychiatric Association 1994), we can begin to understand the cases of familicide committed by men that are the subject of this study. For an individual who has not achieved individuation, separation and divorce arouse significant fears of abandonment, with resulting rage and emotional regression, and an inability to discriminate between the self and the love object. This in turn can precipitate instability of mood, abuse, violence, and homicidal or suicidal behaviours. Possibly the perpetrators' lack of individuation caused them to experience extreme fear when they perceived themselves as emotionally abandoned. The resultant rage and emotional regression, along with the obsessive need to control both partner and children, resulted in the homicide–suicide. In some cases it appears that the children's death was also intended to be the man's ultimate revenge on his wife for leaving him.

In what is still primarily a patriarchal society, a man through his upbringing or socialisation may come to believe that he has certain rights over women simply based on his gender; he may perceive his children to be possessions; and he may think that when experiencing emotional pain it is not an option to seek help. In this situation it is not difficult to see how a build-up of rage and other emotions triggered by a marital breakdown can culminate in homicide–suicide.

IMPLICATIONS FOR POLICY

The study highlights implications for policy, practice and for further research.

As many other studies in the area of domestic violence have found, community agencies and their employees who deal with domestic violence, relationship counselling, divorce and separation, often lack awareness of family violence in all its forms. There are isolated attempts at co-operation between agencies, but their success often depends on individuals within the organisations. Even where there are reciprocal policies and protocols on co-operation and the sharing of information, discussions with refuge staff, for example, reveal that these are not applied universally. It is clearly not sufficient to draw up policies; there must also be processes to ensure and monitor that the policies are adequately resourced and applied.

The legal system in Australia is based on an adversarial approach, in which all 'men' are assumed equal. Cases are rationally argued in order to seek a solution to a dispute or assign responsibility for an anti-social action. It is, therefore, not surprising that the legal system is inadequate in helping women disclose the extent of violence and threats to which they and their children are exposed. There is, generally, a lack of recognition of the power imbalance between women who have been abused and their abuser. Compounding this, a separating couple are often highly emotional, a situation which is not conducive for logic and reason.

Where women in this study did disclose abuse to their legal representatives in the Family Court, they were advised that disclosure could disadvantage them unless they had irrefutable evidence of harm caused by the violence. There are seldom outside witnesses to violence that occurs within the family, and women do not typically seek help for injuries received as a result of their husband's abuse. It is very unlikely that women will provide irrefutable evidence of domestic violence while in the presence of the abuser. The requirement to do so demonstrates ignorance of the dynamics in domestic violence, and compounds the problems experienced by women seeking any legal remedy for their situation. Courts of Petty Sessions have a reputation among women and helping professionals for inconsistency in relation to Violence Restraining Orders—in granting them, in allowing them to lapse, and in dealing with breaches.

The legal system needs to remedy this by ensuring that judicial officers and lawyers receive thorough, continuing training in relation to domestic violence. It needs to devise policies that allow for the difficulties women face in presenting their experience of abuse to the court in the presence of the abuser. These need to translate into practices that redress the power imbalance in any case involving domestic violence before the courts.

Where a threat has been made to harm, it is important this should incur consequences. There is a strong argument that the author of such threats should be made to undergo risk assessment, and any recommended treatment. Thus the risk could be accurately determined, suitable orders drawn up, and appropriate services provided.

It is clear the police still need to develop more effective ways of responding to domestic violence, especially after couples have separated. Particular vigilance is needed where there are indications of deterioration in the mental state of a man following a marital separation, especially when he engages in stalking and other types of harassment.

Police officers currently are trained to intervene in domestic violence, but they also need to learn about risk factors to help them to make decisions in these emotionally volatile situations. They should be diligent about recording and sharing information with colleagues, so that information passes from one shift to another, and to the new district if the family moves. It is important not to treat each incident as a one-off. A composite picture will provide more information to base decisions on when police are called to the next incident. Police and other community agencies should routinely share information about domestic violence; communication should not depend on individuals within each agency. Again, processes need to be set in place so that this occurs.

IMPLICATIONS FOR PRACTICE

This study found that agencies dealing with families need to be more aware of danger signs, and the community generally needs to be educated about domestic violence and related issues. In most of the cases in the study, the risks were very obvious. They included a history of violence, stalking behaviour, threats to harm, rehearsal of the offence, and refusal to accept the finality of separation. In some cases it became evident after the offence that friends and family members knew of these danger signs but did not act on them. If community members had passed this information to the authorities, and if the information was then shared among relevant agencies, some of these children might not have died.

Practical methods for collaboration between agencies and joint case planning need to be standardised, implemented and monitored. All family members need to be provided with counselling programs at a reasonable cost, both to effect behavioural change in perpetrators and to help victims deal with the trauma.

It appears that men continue to have difficulty finding their way to counselling services. This historical problem needs to be tackled as part of community mental health programs. None of the men in this study appeared to be linked into counselling, which might have supported them through the separation process.

There is a serious gap in men's programs, particularly those that help men to deal with marital separation, anger management and domestic violence. It is urgent to integrate men's domestic violence programs with women's programs so the counsellors working with each of the partners can share information. This would provide a reality check for any apparent treatment gains and enable more effective monitoring of safety.

Community health policy should include educational programs for people suffering emotional crisis of all kinds, but especially relationship breakdowns. Friends and family could also be targeted, with a view to encouraging the individual undergoing the crisis to seek professional help from an appropriate agency, and to encourage those close to them to provide support through the crisis.

There is also a need for the community as a whole, not just family and friends, to share the responsibility for the safety of its vulnerable members, and to learn about domestic violence and the dangers that some families face in marital separation. It is clear in some of the cases involved in this study that community members did have knowledge of threats to harm, or of behaviour indicating serious risk to children. Yet this knowledge was not communicated to those who could have taken preventive action.

Services to victims could be improved by extending offers of assistance past the initial crisis, perhaps with a regular follow-up for at least a year after the offence. Hours should be extended, as respondents mentioned difficulty in sleeping, the need for counselling support in the early hours of the morning, and the restricted services available outside office hours.

Clearly courts should pay more attention to the safety of children who are having contact with a parent who has been violent towards his spouse, even though there is no evidence of the children having been harmed. Where agencies identify risk factors in a family, they must find more effective ways of sharing information.

The families of the perpetrators of familicide are neglected; a comprehensive service needs to be set up for them. As we have seen, the Victim Support Service does not contact these families because it perceives itself to have a conflict of interest. These families share the loss of the children and experience similar grief to members of the maternal families, as well as coping with the loss of their son and brother and knowing that he was responsible for this awful crime. Existing counselling agencies will find it difficult to meet the special needs of these families. A specialist agency, or specialist training for counsellors, is needed to provide service to this overlooked group.

PREVENTION AND FURTHER RESEARCH

Besides the measures suggested so far, the courts could intervene more effectively in high-risk cases. They need to accept therapeutic jurisprudence as a model for service delivery wherever there is evidence of family violence, child abuse, substance abuse or mental illness. Therapeutic jurisprudence is a philosophy in law which favours outcomes that enhance the general well-being of litigants and the community, rather than a purely legalistic solution. This emphasis would provide a strong opportunity to develop early intervention services focusing on prevention.

The Family Court of Western Australia currently operates an innovative diversion program named Columbus. It deals with cases where there are allegations of family violence or child abuse. In contrast to the Magellan project in Victoria and the ACT, which deals only with child abuse, Columbus provides for differential case management and is more expansive. Such programs may be expanded to incorporate other areas of family dysfunction, substance abuse, and mental illness, where a purely legal solution is unlikely to be adequate.

Further research is urgently needed to expand knowledge of familicide and associated risk factors. In particular, research on family homicide–suicide following separation, or perceived loss of a relationship, should look at the early life experiences of perpetrators to uncover information about their motivation. Factors relating to the perpetrator, such as his criminal record, history of substance abuse or mental illness, sexually abusive behaviour, stalking or violence, and whether or not he had a family history of child abuse, are all worthy of study, and could lead to new understandings about how these offences occur. Once motivation and causal factors are better understood, it may be possible to screen for high-risk cases and intervene with treatment to prevent the offence.

Further research is needed on the effects of familicide on all family members, including the paternal family, and on workers in the courts, police and community agencies who are involved with familicide. This will identify the gaps in services currently provided.

As a student of social work more than twenty-five years ago, I remember learning that a civilised society can be judged by the way in which its most vulnerable citizens are treated. Each man, woman or child who dies as a result of familicide, or any other form of domestic violence, testifies to our failure as a community to safeguard our most vulnerable members, be they children, the disempowered, or those whose emotional or mental state puts them at risk.

Some domestic violence and men's programs have become polarised around gender issues. I believe this tendency works against the long-term safety and well-being of children in our community. Many workers in the area now recognise the need to tackle this issue, while maintaining safety and confidentiality for their clients. In the last few years it has been heartening to see the growth of communication between agencies, and a collaborative approach developing in meeting the needs of families affected by violence. However, this is just a beginning. As I move between agencies and meet and talk with workers, I see that their commitment to improving the lives of all their clients, especially the children, keeps them involved in what must surely be one of the most difficult areas of service delivery to families.

I believe these caring and dedicated people, with the support of the community and an open-minded, open-handed government, will eventually create an Australia where the heart of the family, the home, is a truly safe and nurturing place for all its members. Then Australia may be able to judge itself (and hopefully be judged by others) as a civilised society.

Appendix 1: Information Sheet

FAMILICIDE IN DISPUTED CUSTODY/ACCESS CASES

At regular intervals multiple murders are committed within families, where custody of or access to children is in dispute.

Little is known of the reasons why these offences occur, and therefore no methods of trying to prevent them currently exist. If information can be gained from the survivors of these offences, or from members of their families, our knowledge of how and why these offences occur will be expanded and thus ultimately preventive strategies may be devised.

It is intended that information from a number of different sources, including interviews with survivors and their families will be used in order to establish common factors that exist in these cases prior to the offences being committed. The acquisition of this knowledge is the first step in gaining understanding of why these offences occur and in ultimate prevention.

I invite you to ask any questions you wish regarding this research project and should you wish to withdraw your consent to further participate, you are free to do so at any time, without prejudice in any way. In this case, all records of my contact with you will be destroyed.

It is acknowledged that discussing these tragedies is certain to be distressing to interviewees therefore this research is being conducted with the co-operation of the Victim Support Service, which is available to provide counselling should it be required subsequent to the interview. The Victim Support Service may be contacted on 08-9221-0444. Freecall 1800-818-988.

CAROLYN JOHNSON Researcher   (Tel. Contact No.)

Appendix 2: Consent Form

FAMILICIDE IN DISPUTED CUSTODY/ACCESS CASES

I_____ of_____(street)

_____(suburb or town)
hereby agree to be interviewed regarding my personal experience of
murder within the family. I have read the Information Sheet and any
questions I had have been answered to my satisfaction.

I agree to participate in this activity, realising that I may withdraw at any
time without prejudice. I understand that all information provided is
treated as strictly confidential and will not be releasd by the investigator
unless required to do so by law. I agree that research data gathered for the
study may be published provided my name and other identifying information is not used.

The Committee for Human Rights at The University of Western Australia
requires that all participants are informed that if they have any complaint
regarding the manner in which a research project is conducted, it may
be given to the researcher or, alternatively to the Secretary, Committee
for Human Rights, Registrar's Office, The University of Western Australia,
Nedlands, WA 6907 (Tel. No. 9380-3703). All study participants will be
provided with a copy of the Information Sheet and Consent Form for their
personal record.

_____(participant)_____(researcher)

_____(date)   _____(date)

CAROLYN JOHNSON Researcher   (Tel. Contact No.)

Appendix 3: Interview Schedule

FAMILICIDE IN DISPUTED CUSTODY/ACCESS CASES

1   What was the status of the relationship at time of offence?
2   What was the relationship of the victims?
3   Was there a current court process?
4   What was the nature of the court dispute?
5   What stage was the court process at?
6   Had the parties attended the Family Court Counselling Service?
7   How many times?
8   Was there a current court order or deed of agreement at the time of the offence?
9   What were the circumstances of the relationship breakdown?
10   Had there been a history of violence in the relationship?
10a   Had there been a history of sexual abuse in the relationship?
11   Had violence got better or worse since separation?
12   Had there been a previous history of depressive or other psychiatric illness?
13   Had there been a recent history of depressive or psychiatric illness prior to the offence?
14   Had there been previous threats made by the perpetrator in relation to the safety of family members?
15   Had there been previous threats made by the perpetrator in relation to his own safety?
16   What community agencies were involved with the family prior to the offence?
17   What were the circumstances leading up to the offence?
18   What could have been done to avoid this offence:
    a   by the court?
    b   by the Family Court Counselling Service?
    c   by other community agencies?
    d   by the police?

19   Was help available to your family after the offence?
20   What help should be available to families after such an offence?
21   Is there anything else you think I should know about this?
22   Is there anyone else you think I should talk to in gathering
       information about this?
23   How do you explain what happened?
24   How do members of your family explain it?
25   How do members of his family explain it?
26   What effect has it had on you and your family?

Glossary

Some general terms are used in this book in a specific sense, as explained here.

Access: the time spent by the non-custodial parent with their child or children. *See* **contact.**

Child: a child or children of either or both parents, including biological and adopted children and stepchildren.

Consent Order: a court order based on the consent of the parties.

Contact: the preferred term in Australian family law for access, not yet in general use.

Contact parent: the preferred term in Australian family law for a non-custodial parent.

Custodial parent: the parent with whom the child lives. *See* **residential parent.**

Custody: the right of a parent to have the child of the relationship live with them. *See* **residency.**

Decree Absolute: the final order for divorce issued by the court, which allows the parties to remarry.

Decree Nisi: the provisional order for divorce granted by the court, which becomes a Decree Absolute unless cause is shown to the contrary.

Deed of Agreement: a legal document drawn up by the parties, which is then registered by the court as a legally binding agreement. It has the same legal weight as a court order. Typically, it is drawn up where a couple are not experiencing high levels of conflict and wish to avoid the time and expense of seeking a court solution to where and when the children should reside with each parent.

Disputed residency and contact: a disagreement between parents about where their child should live and what arrangements should be made for contact with the parent they do not live with. *See* **residency.**

Familicide: where a person kills a member or members of his or her own family and then attempts or commits suicide.

Femicide: the killing of an adult woman.

Filicide: the killing of a child by a parent, step-parent or de facto parent.

Homicide: the intentional killing of one human being by another.

Interim Minute of Consent Orders: a court order made by agreement between the parties for an interim period, usually pending the next court appearance.

Minute of Consent Orders: a court order made by agreement between the parties.

Murder–suicide: homicide where the perpetrator takes his or her own life shortly after killing the victim/s.

Non-custodial parent: a parent with whom a child does not reside. *See* **contact parent; residential parent.**

Recovery Order: a court order to hand up (relinquish) a child.

Residency: the preferred term in Australian family law for custody, not yet in general use.

Residential parent: a parent with whom a child resides. *See* **custodial parent; residency.**

Spousal relationship: a relationship of sexual intimates currently or previously cohabiting, whether legally married or in a de facto relationship.

Survivors: people who have lived through the trauma of having a child in their family murdered by a family member.

Select Bibliography

Alder, C. & Polk, K. (2001) *Child Victims of Homicide*, Cambridge University Press, Cambridge.

Allen, N. (1980) *Homicide*, Human Sciences Press, New York and London.

—— (1983) 'Homicide Followed by Suicide, 1970–1979', *Suicide and Life-Threatening Behavior*, vol. 13 (3): 155–65.

American Psychiatric Association (1994) *Diagnostic and Statistical Manual of Mental Disorders, Fourth Edition* [*DSM-IV*], Washington, DC.

Ammerman, R. & Hersen, M., eds (1992) *Assessment of Family Violence*, John Wiley & Sons, New York.

Australian Bureau of Statistics (2002a) *Suicides, Recent Trends, Australia*, Cat. No. 3309.0.55.001.

—— (2002b) *Causes of Death, Australia: Underlying Causes of Death, State of Usual Residence and IC10 for 2001*, Cat. No. 3303.0.

Australian Institute of Criminology (2003) 'Homicide victimisation rates per 100,000 population: Australia, states and territories, 1 July 1989 – 30 June 2002', National Homicide Monitoring Program, Canberra, Australia, <http://www.aic.gov.au/research/homicide/stats/hvr.html> accessed 14 July 2004.

Bailey, K. (1987) *Methods of Social Research*, Macmillan, New York.

Baron-Cohen, S., ed. (1997) *The Maladapted Mind*, Psychology Press, East Sussex.

Becker, J. V. and Abel, G. G. (1978) 'Men and the Victimisation of Women', in J. Chapman and M. Gates, eds, *The Victimisation of Women*, Sage Publications, Beverly Hills, 1978: 29–52.

Biddulph, S. (1994) *Manhood*, Finch Publishing, Sydney.

Bonney, R. (1998) *Homicide II*, New South Wales Bureau of Crime Statistics and Research, Sydney.

Carcach, C. & Grabosky, P. N. (1998) *Murder–Suicide in Australia*, Trends and Issues in Crime and Criminal Justice No. 82, Australian Institute of Criminology, Canberra.

Carcach, C. & James, M. (1998) *Homicide Between Intimate Partners*, Trends and Issues in Crime and Criminal Justice No. 90, Australian Institute of Criminology, Canberra.

Chafetz, J.(1988) *Feminist Sociology*, Peacock, Illinois.

Chapman, J. & Gates, M., eds (1978) *The Victimisation of Women*, Sage Publications, Beverly Hills.

Curtis, L. A. (1974) *Criminal Violence*, Lexington Books, Massachusetts in A. Wallace (1986) *Homicide: The Social Reality*, New South Wales Bureau of Crime Statistics, Sydney.

Daly, M. & Wilson, M. (1988), *Homicide*, Aldine de Gruyter, New York.

Deaton, W. S. & Hertica, M. (2001) *Growing Free: A Manual for Survivors of Domestic Violence*, Haworth Maltreatment and Trauma Press, New York.

Denzin, N. & Lincoln, Y. (1994) *Handbook of Qualitative Research*, Sage Publications, Beverly Hills.

D'orban, P. T. (1979) 'Women who kill their children', *British Journal of Psychiatry* 134: 560–71 in A. Wilczynski (1997) *Child Homicide*, Oxford University Press, London.

Durkheim, E. (1968) *Suicide, A Study in Sociology*, trans. J. A. Spaulding & G. Simpson, Routledge & Kegan Paul, London.

Easteal, P. W. (1993) *Killing the Beloved*, Australian Institute of Criminology, Canberra.

Edwards, S. (1985) 'A socio-legal evaluation of gender ideologies in domestic violence assaults and spousal homicides', *Victimology: An International Journal*, vol. 10 no. 1–4: 186–205 in P. W. Easteal (1993) *Killing the Beloved*, Australian Institute of Criminology, Canberra.

Elliott and Shanahan Research (1988) 'Summary of Background Research for the Development of a Campaign Against Domestic

Violence', Department of the Prime Minister and Cabinet, Canberra.

Ewing, C. (1987) *Battered Women Who Kill: Psychological Self-Defence as Legal Justification*, Lexington Books, Lexington, Mass.

—— (1997) *Fatal Families: The Dynamics of Intrafamilial Homicide*, Sage Publications, Beverly Hills.

Finkelhor, Gelles, Hotaling & Straus, eds (1983) *The Dark Side of Families*, Sage Publications, Beverly Hills.

Gates, M. (1978) 'Introduction' in J. Chapman and M. Gates, eds, *The Victimisation of Women*, Sage Publications, Beverley Hills, 1978: 9.

Gelles, R. J. (1987) *The Violent Home*, Sage Publications, Beverly Hills.

Gilmore, D. D. (1990) *Manhood in the Making: Cultural Concepts of Masculinity*, Yale University Press, New Haven cited in K. Polk (1994) *When Men Kill*, Cambridge University Press, Cambridge.

Hore, E., Gibson, J. & Bordow, S. (1996) *Domestic Homicide*, Family Court of Australia, Victoria.

James, M. & Carcach, C. (1997) *Homicide in Australia, 1989–96*, Australian Institute of Criminology, Griffith, ACT.

Jenkins, A. (1993) *Invitations to Responsibility*, Dulwich Centre Publications, Adelaide.

Johnson, C. (2002) 'Familicide and Disputed Residency and Contact in Western Australia: A Contemporary Picture', unpublished MA thesis, The University of Western Australia, Perth.

Jones, A. (1996) *Women Who Kill*, Beacon Press, Boston.

Jordan, P. (1985) *The Effects of Marital Separation on Men*, Family Court of Australia, Research Report No. 6.

Lansky, M. (1992) *Fathers Who Fail*, The Analytic Press, Hillsdale, NJ.

Lester, D. (1986) *The Murderer and His Murder*, AMS Press, New York.

Lunde, D. T. (1975) *Murder and Madness*, Stanford Alumni Press, Stanford, Calif.

Mann, C. R. (1996) *When Women Kill*, State University of New York Press, Albany, NY.

Martin, D. (1978) 'Battered Women: Society's Problem', in J. Chapman and M. Gates, eds, *The Victimisation of Women*, Sage Publications, Beverly Hills, 1978: 111.

Monahan, J. (1981) *Predicting Violent Behaviour*, Sage Publications, Beverly Hills.

Mouzos, J. (1999a) *Femicide: The Killing of Women in Australia, 1989–1998*, Australian Institute of Criminology, Canberra.

—— (1999b) *Mental Disorder and Homicide in Australia*, Trends and Issues in Crime and Criminal Justice No. 133, Australian Institute of Criminology, Canberra.

—— (2000) *Homicidal Encounters: A Study of Homicide in Australia, 1989–1999*, Australian Institute of Criminology, Canberra.

—— (2002) *Homicide in Australia, 2000–2001*, National Homicide Monitoring Program Annual Report, Australian Institute of Criminology, Canberra.

Mouzos, J. & Rushforth, C. (2003) *Family Homicide in Australia*, Australian Institute of Criminology, Canberra.

Muller, R. J. (1994) *Anatomy of a Splitting Borderline*, Praeger, Connecticut and London.

Naylor, B. & Neale, D. (1988) *Domestic Homicide*, Victorian Law Reform Commission, Melbourne.

O'Donnell, C. & Craney, J. (1982) *Family Violence in Australia*, Longman Cheshire, Melbourne.

Phillips, B. (1971) *Social Research Strategy and Tactics*, Macmillan, New York.

Polk, K. (1994) *When Men Kill*, Cambridge University Press, Cambridge.

Pritchard, C. (1995) *Suicide, the Ultimate Rejection: A Psycho-Social Study*, Open University Press, Philadelphia.

Radford, J. & Russell, D., eds (1992) *Femicide: The Politics of Woman Killing*, Twayne Publishers, New York.

Rasche, C. E. (1989) 'Stated and attributed motives for lethal violence in intimate relationships 1980', paper delivered at the American Society of Criminology, Reno in K. Polk (1994) *When Men Kill*, Cambridge University Press, Cambridge.

Resnick, P. J. (1969) 'Child Murder by Parents: A Psychiatric Review of Filicide', *American Journal of Psychiatry* 126: 73–82 cited in A. Wilczynski, *Child Homicide*, Oxford University Press, London, 1997: 45.

Retterstol, N. (1993) *Suicide: A European Perspective*, Cambridge University Press, Cambridge.

Saakvitne, K. & Pearlman, L. A. (1996) *Transforming the Pain*, W. W. Norton & Co., New York.

Schneidman, E. S., ed. (1976) *Suicidology: Contemporary Developments*, Grune & Stratton, New York.

—— (1993) *Suicide as Psychache: A Clinical Approach to Self-Destructive Behavior*, Jason Aronson, Northvale, NJ.

Silverman, R. & Mukherjee, S. K. (1987) 'Intimate Homicide: An Analysis of Violent Social Relationships', *Behavioral Sciences and the Law*, vol. 5 (1): 37–47.

Stack, S. (1997) 'Homicide followed by Suicide: An Analysis of Chicago data', Criminology, vol. 35 (3): 435–54.

Strang, H. (1991) *Homicides in Australia, 1989–90*, Australian Institute of Criminology, Canberra.

—— (1993) *Homicides in Australia, 1991–92*, Australian Institute of Criminology, Canberra.

Strang, H. & Gerull, S., eds (1993) *Homicide: Patterns, Prevention and Control*, Australian Institute of Criminology, Canberra.

United States Department of Justice Website <www.ojp.usdoj.gov/bjs/homicide/intimates.htm> accessed 14 July 2004.

Wallace, A. (1986) *Homicide: The Social Reality*, New South Wales Bureau of Crime Statistics, Sydney.

Websdale, N. (1999) *Understanding Domestic Homicide*, Northeastern University Press, Boston.

West, D. J. (1965) *Murder Followed by Suicide*, Heinemann, London.

Western Australian Government (1986) *Report of the Task Force on Domestic Violence*, Breaking the Silence: Report to the Western Australian Government, Perth.

Wilczynski, A. (1997) *Child Homicide*, Oxford University Press, London.

Wilson, M. & Daly, M. (1992) 'The Man Who Mistook His Wife for a Chattel' in J. Barkow, L. Cosmides and J. Tooby, eds, *The Adapted Mind*, Oxford University Press, London, pp. 243–76; cited in 'Till Death Us Do Part' in J. Radford and D. Russell, eds,

Femicide: The Politics of Woman Killing, Twayne Publishers, New York, 1992: 85.

Wilson, P. R. (1985) *Murder of the Innocents*, Rigby, Adelaide.

Wolfgang, M. (1958) *Patterns of Criminal Homicide*, University of Philadelphia Press, Philadelphia.

Women's Coalition Against Family Violence (1994) *Blood on Whose Hands?* Victorian Women's Trust, Australia.

Index

154